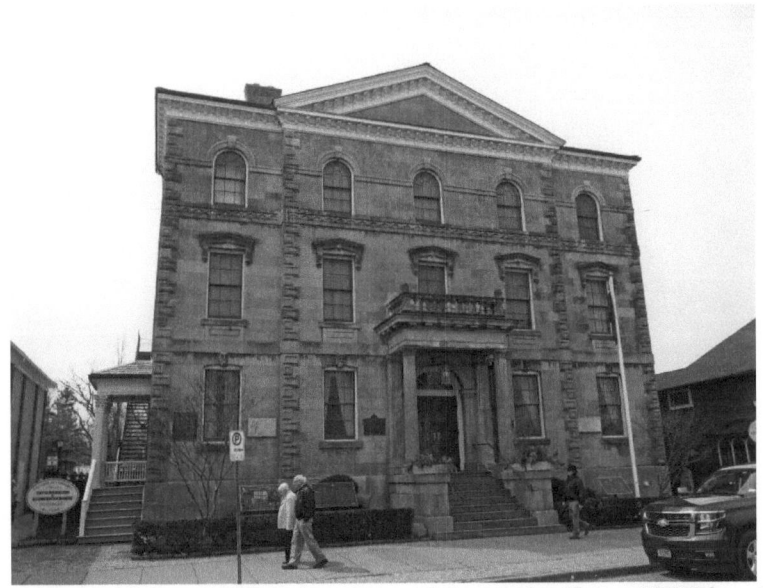

26 Queen Street – Niagara Court House built in 1847 for the united counties of Lincoln, Welland and Haldimand - This is the third and only surviving court house erected for the former Niagara district. Constructed between 1846 and 1848, it is in the Neo-classical style. Though the courts were moved to St. Catharines in 1862, this building continued to play an important role in the life of the community. It served as the Town Hall and later as the founding home of the Shaw Festival.

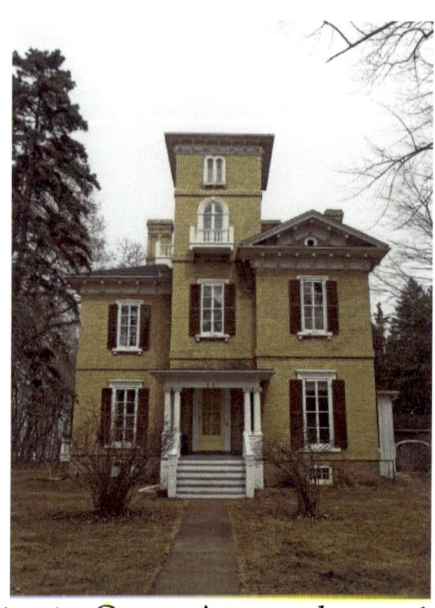

17 Byron Street – Queen Anne style, cornice brackets, pediment, tower, third-storey balconies, ionic capitals

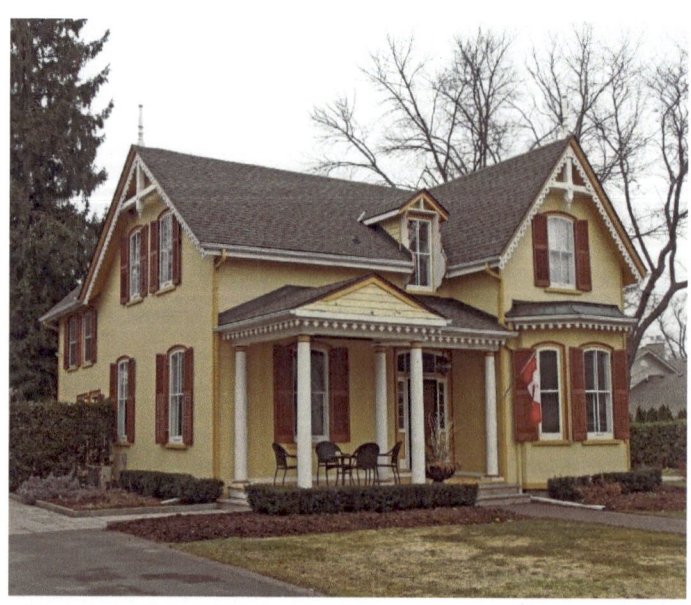

Victoria Street – Marrakech Mansion – Gothic Revival, verge board trim on gables, pediment, bay window – Book 2

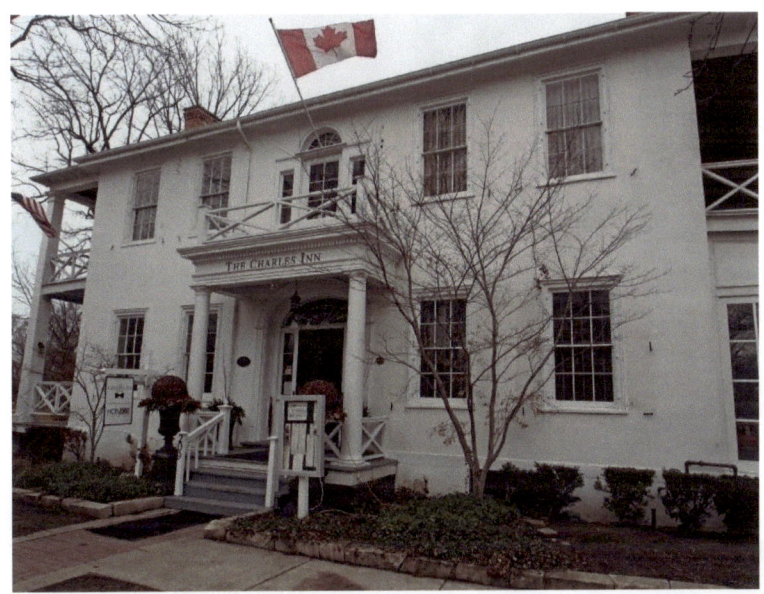

209 Queen Street - The Charles Inn c. 1832 – Georgian style – The house was constructed in 1832 by Charles Richardson, a barrister and Member of Parliament. He used the house as his principle residence and later as his summer house. -Book 1

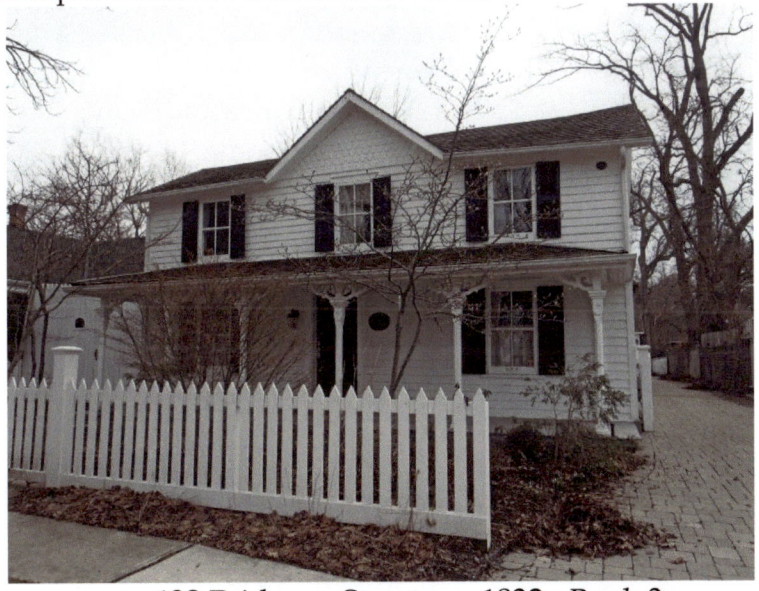

132 Prideaux Street – c. 1832 - Book 3

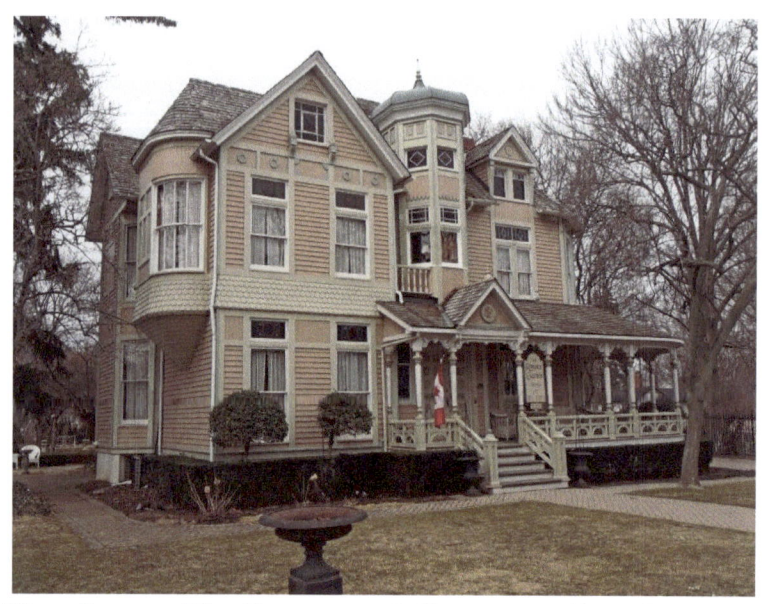

177 King Street – The Romance Collection Gallery featuring the exclusive works of Trisha Romance and Tanya Jean Peterson – Queen Anne style home – Book 2

Harriston and Clifford, Ontario – My Top 7 Picks

Harriston is a community in Wellington County located at the headwaters of the Maitland River. In the summer of 1845, the first non-Aboriginal settlers arrived in the area and the Crown made land available for sale in the region in 1854.

The town was named after Archibald Harrison, a Toronto farmer who was granted land along the Maitland River in 1854. Harrison's brothers George and Joshua built several mills in the area and the community soon grew.

A post office was established in 1856. The southern road leading to Harriston was graveled in 1861, opening easier access to the larger markets of Guelph, Hamilton, and Toronto. By 1867, the village contained many businesses including wagon works and blacksmith shops.

The town became a prosperous commercial and farm-implement manufacturing center following the construction of the Wellington Grey and Bruce Railway, completed to Harriston in 1871. A telegraph link to the community followed soon after. A second rail line, the Toronto, Grey and Bruce Railway, intersected the village in 1873.

Harriston was incorporated as a village in 1872, and as a town in 1878. In 1882, the Grand Trunk Railway began shipping through Harriston. A Carnegie Library opened in Harriston in 1908.

Beginning in the late 1860s, Harriston's citizens began to create friendly service organizations parallel to, as well as outside, of religious groups. In 1868, the Loyal Orange Institution opened a Harriston Lodge; in 1871, the Freemasons established a Lodge. Other groups followed, such as the Independent Order of Oddfellows (1879), and the

Independent Order of Good Templars (active by 1874) and the Royal Templars of Temperance (active by 1900).

The Harriston Minto Agricultural Society was founded in 1859 and continues to operate an annual fall fair on the third weekend in September.

Clifford is a community in the Town of Minto in Wellington County. The village of Clifford was founded around 1855 as Minto Village. After the opening of the post office in 1856, the settlement was renamed Clifford by the first postmaster Francis Brown after Clifford in West Yorkshire, England. Clifford was incorporated as a village in 1873.

Clifford is home to Wightman Telecom. The Wightman family has owned and operated a communication system in Clifford since 1908. The company is now involved in high speed fiber-optic internet, cable, and telephone throughout mid-western Ontario.

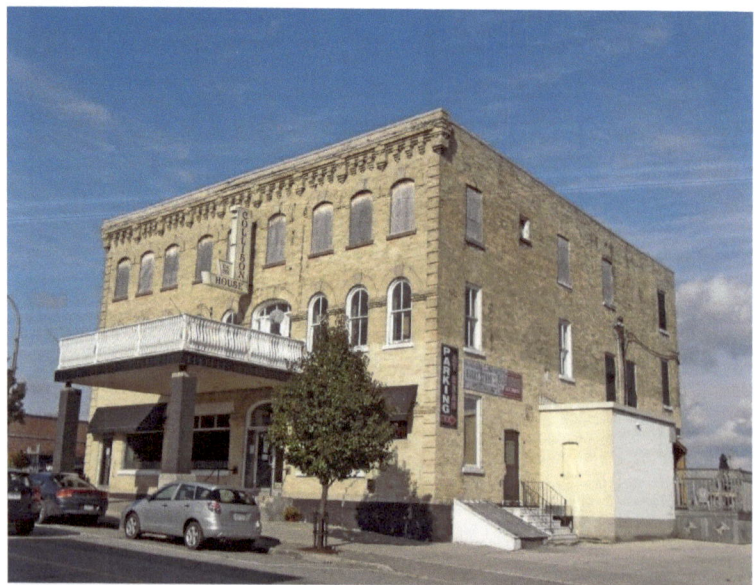

Harriston – Collison House, established 1876 - beveled dentil molding, corner quoins, balcony above entrance, yellow brick

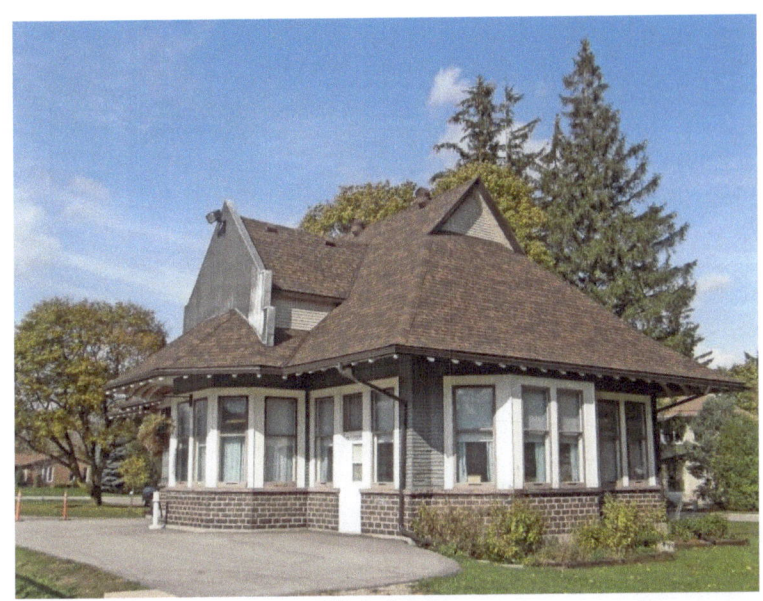

Harriston

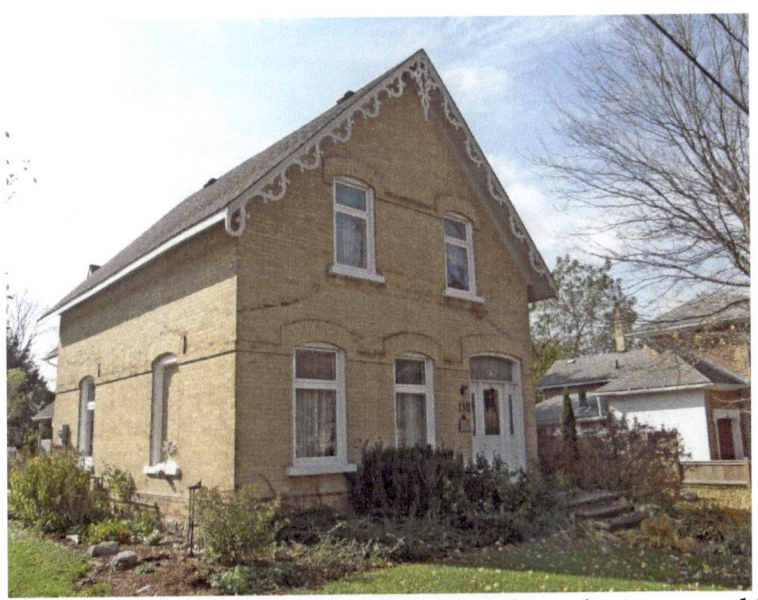

138 Elora Street – Gothic Revival, verge board trim on gable - William Gordon, Cheesemaker – 1875

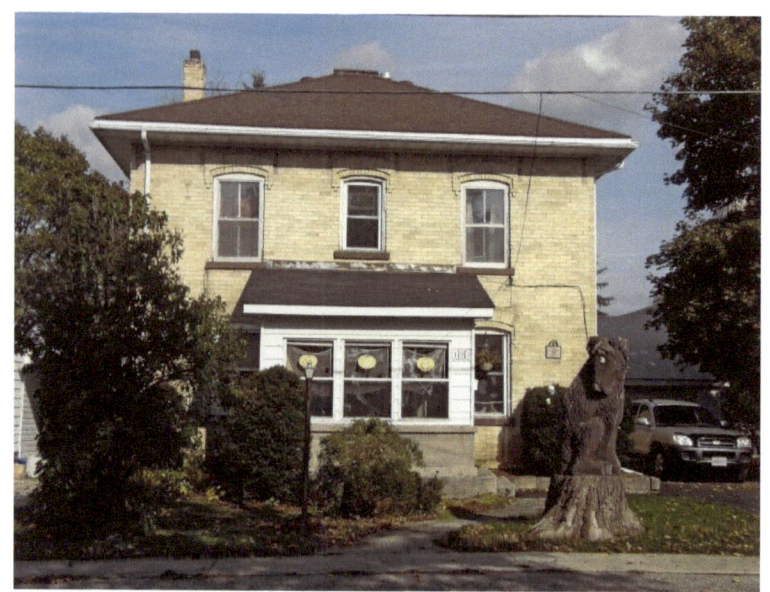

Harriston - #123 – Alexander McDougall, Contractor – 1874
W. A. Harvey, M.D. – 1885 – Italianate, hipped roof

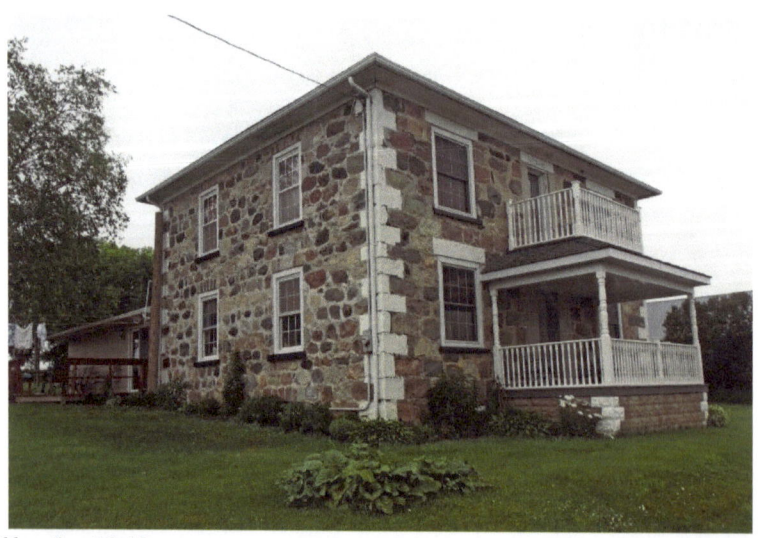

Clifford - 1868 – stone, corner quoins, balcony on second floor

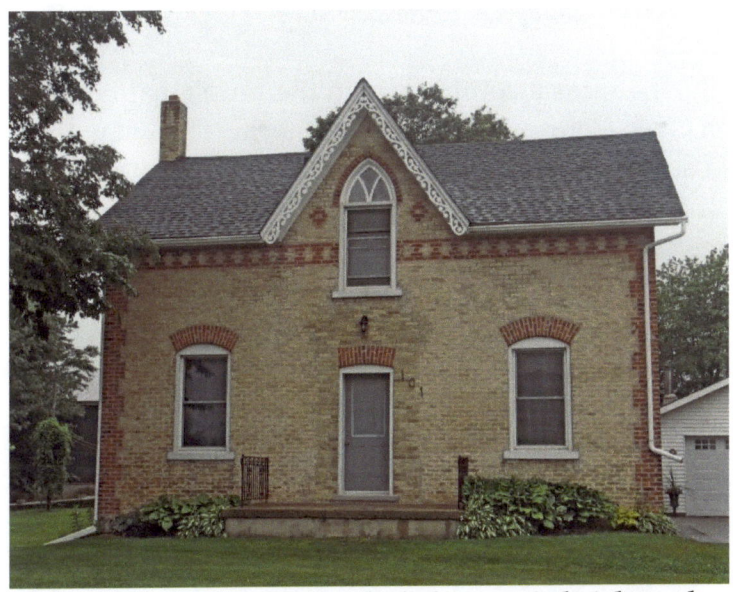

Clifford - #101 - Gothic Revival, dichromatic brickwork, verge board trim

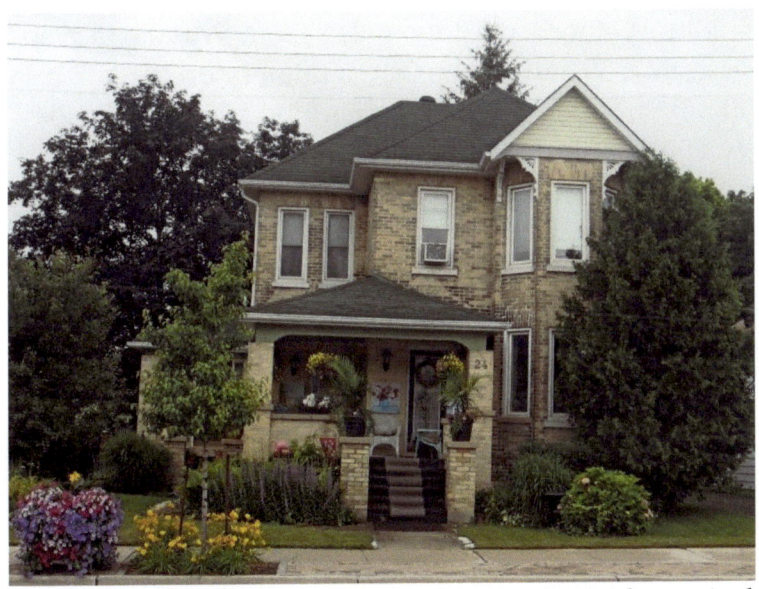

Clifford - 24 Elora Street – fretwork, two-storey bay window

Neustadt, Ontario – My Top 7 Picks

Neustadt is a community in the municipality of West Grey in Grey County in southern Ontario. The village is located south of Hanover on Grey Road 10 and north of Guelph and Kitchener. Neustadt is a picturesque rural Ontario village with German roots and a village history full of vibrant farming culture.

The village's name is of German origin and it translates to "new town". It was founded in 1856 by David Winkler, a settler from Germany. He purchased 400 acres from the government, laid out the town-site, dammed Meux Creek and built a sawmill. A flour mill and grist mill were also erected near the dam the following year. Many other German speaking settlers began arriving immediately. Winkler was the founder of many other institutions, including opening the first post office in town in the year 1857. Later he became a Justice of the Peace and Reeve of Normanby Township.

John Weinert, a saddle maker from Prussia, moved into Neustadt in 1859 and established a tannery on the north side of William Street. By 1861, he had added a boot and shoe factory and supplied footwear to the settlers. Henry Huether, an immigrant from Baden, Germany, constructed a wooden frame Brewery; a fire in 1859 destroyed it. The brewery was reconstructed in fieldstone and reopened in 1869. The brewery continued to be successful until 1916 when it became a creamery. For many years it remained empty until 1997 when it was reopened as Neustadt Springs Brewery which currently brews ten brands of beer.

In the early 1880s, the village saw its peak of development. The opening of a modern school and several new churches, businesses, and industries lead to a growth in population. Many years later, small businesses, farm equipment dealer, creameries, woolen mills, egg grading stations, some stores and later banks began to vanish. Each closure was critical to the village. Fewer attractions meant fewer visitors; the economy and population began to decline. In 2000, the Village of Neustadt with the Townships of Bentinck, Glenelg and Normanby, and the Town of Durham formed the Municipality of West Grey.

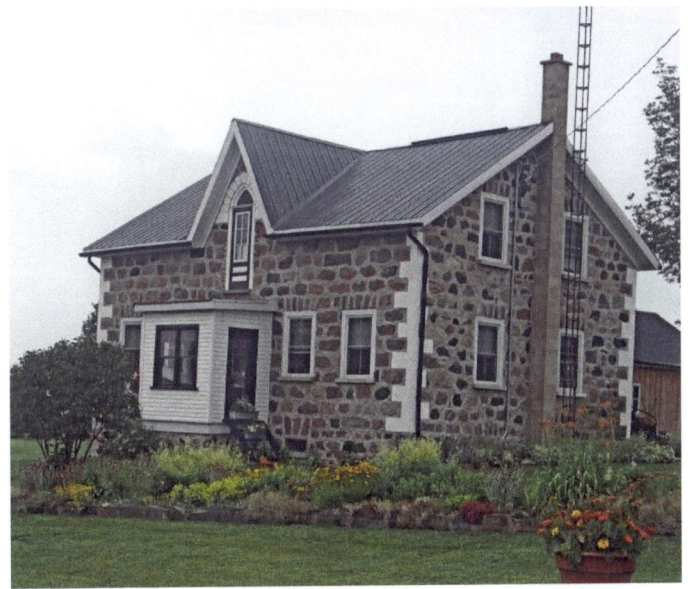

Robert and Janice Polfuss' house – Gothic Revival, stone, corner quoins

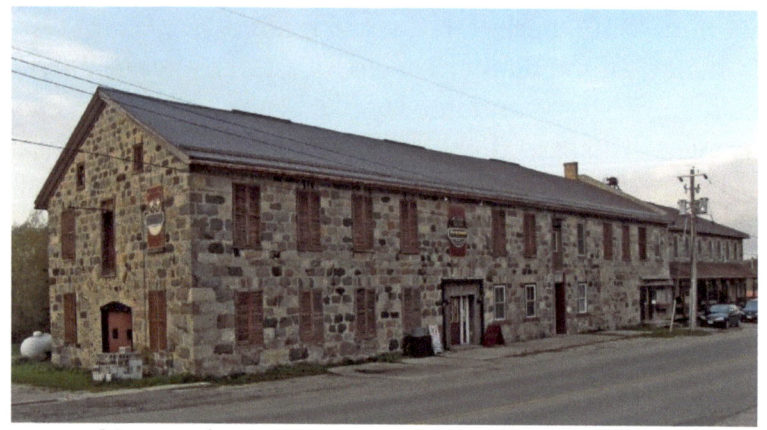

Neustadt Springs Brewery - Gothic, stone

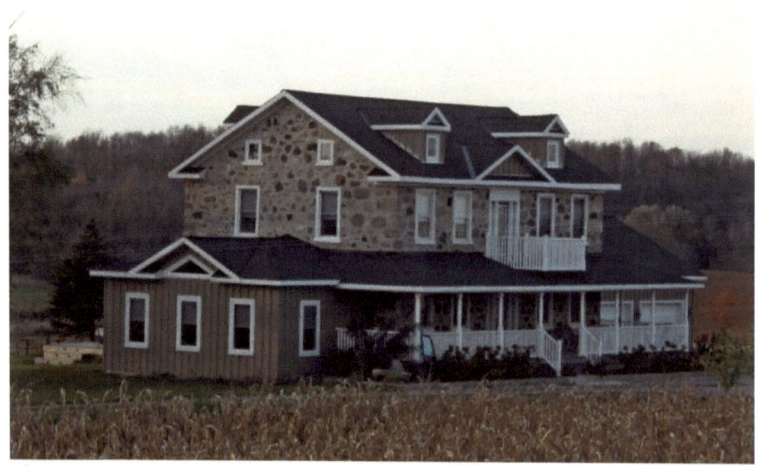

Gothic - stone, cornice return on gable, dormers, balcony on second floor

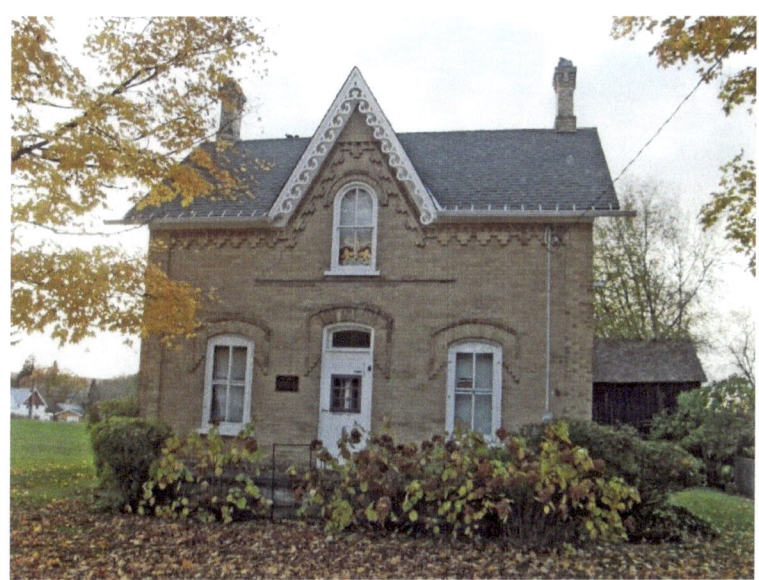

The Right Honorable John Diefenbaker, son of a local school teacher, was born in this house on September 18, 1895. A distinguished Parliamentarian, he was first elected to the House of Commons in 1940 and served as 13th Prime Minister of Canada, 1957-1963. Gothic Revival, verge board on gable.

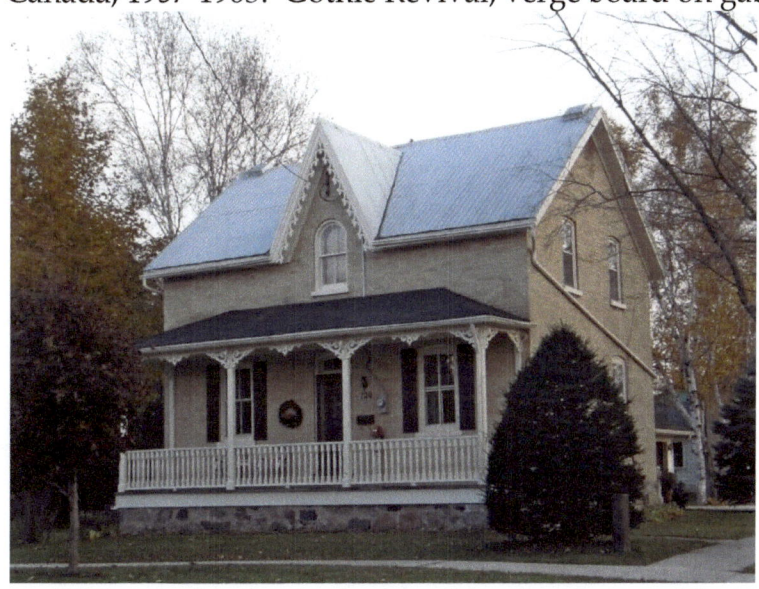

#720 – Gothic Revival, verge board trim on gable

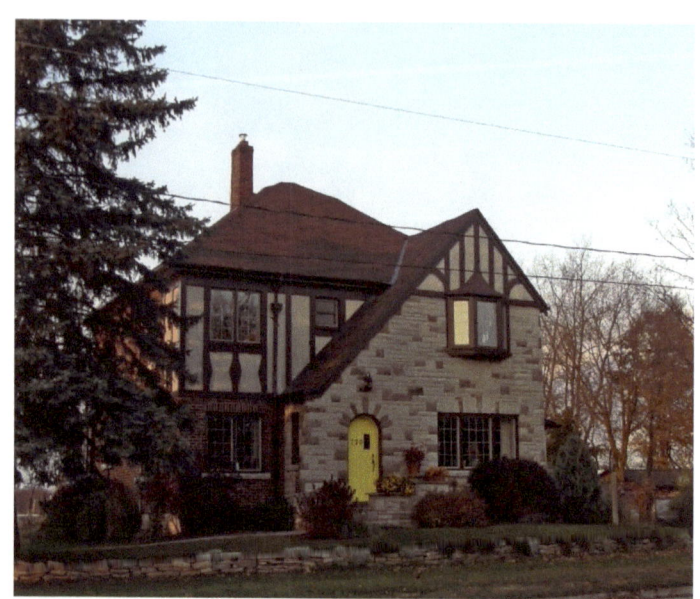
Tudor

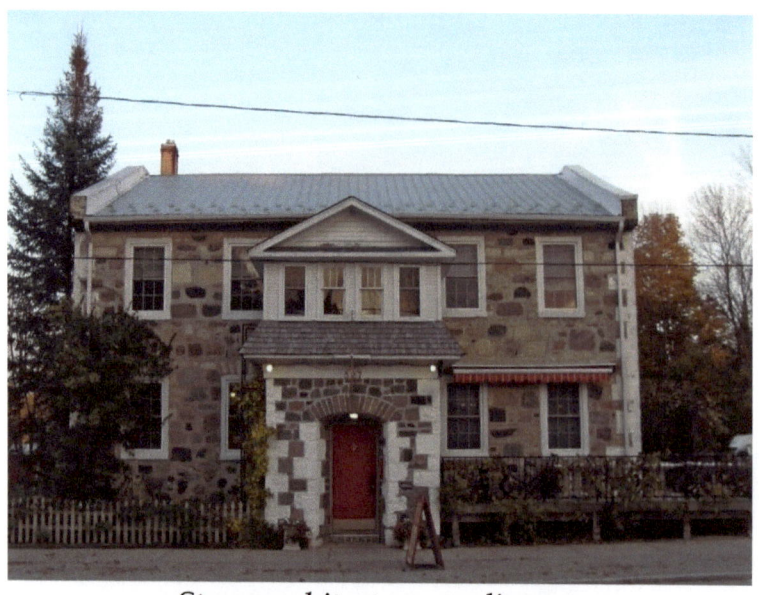
Stone architecture, pediment

Port Elgin, Ontario – My Top 9 Picks

Originally, the village of Port Elgin was named Normanton. In 1873, the community was named after James Bruce, 8th Earl of Elgin, a former Governor-General of the Province of Canada. In the 1990s, Port Elgin was merged into the town of Saugeen Shores. Port Elgin is close to MacGregor Point Provincial Park and Southampton in Bruce County; the community has several beaches on Lake Huron.

In 1854, Benjamin Shantz acquired a sawmill on Mill Creek from George Butchart. Nearby he built a gristmill and within three years a community of 250 people developed around these mills. Stores, hotels and tanneries were built and a village plot for Port Elgin was laid out in 1857. Businessmen Henry Hilker, Samuel Bricker, and John Stafford contributed to the development of the settlement.

The original economic development of Port Elgin during the 19th century was based on its harbor facilities on Lake Huron constructed in 1857–1858. This made the village a distribution center for the surrounding agricultural region. The arrival of the Wellington, Grey and Bruce Railway in 1872 further stimulated the growth of the community. The increasing urbanization of Ontario and the increased importance of the road network for transporting goods resulted in a declining economy and population. More recently, recreation and the nearby Bruce Nuclear Generating Station have dominated the local economy.

The Port Elgin and North Shore Railway is a two foot (610 mm) narrow gauge heritage railway. The railway operates excursion trains along the beach on a one-mile route in downtown Port Elgin. The round trip takes about twenty minutes.

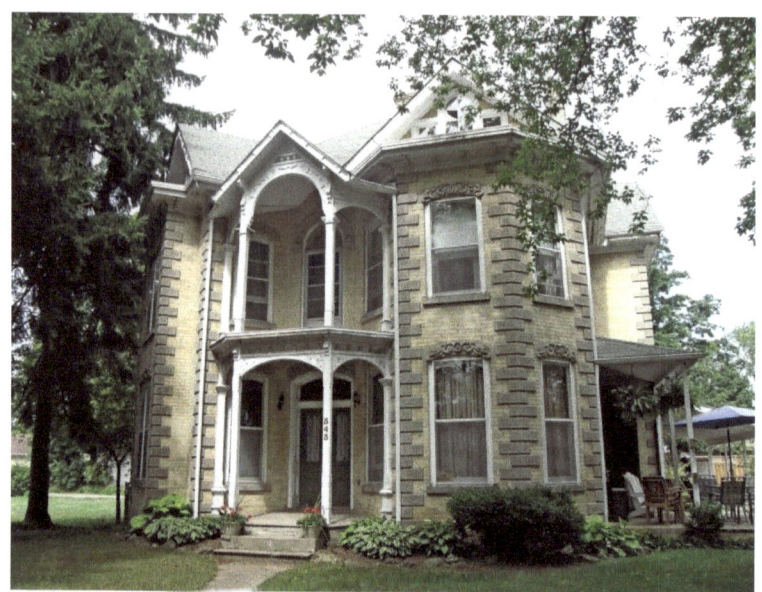

543 Mill Street – Queen Anne style – yellow brick, quoins, Palladian windows in gables, large fretwork pieces resembling brackets on eaves of second floor porch, decorative window hoods

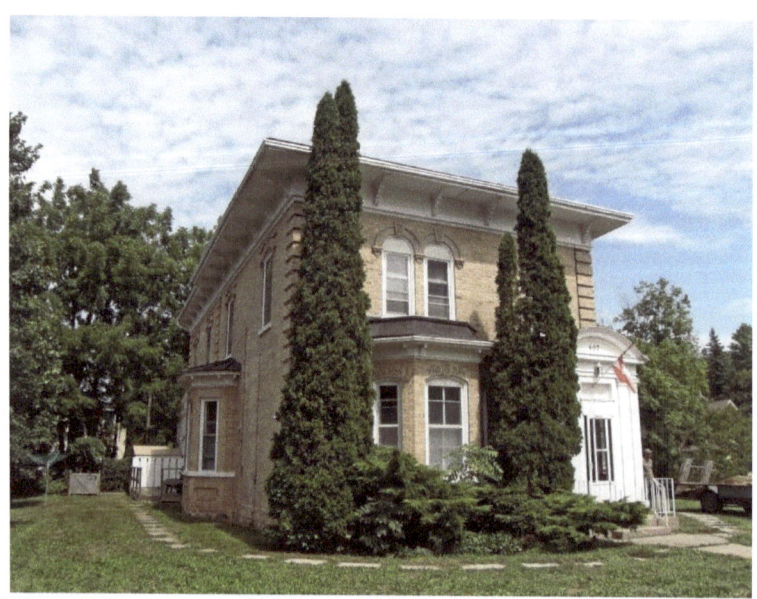

467 Green Street – Italianate style – "Lavrock House" – corner quoins, bay windows

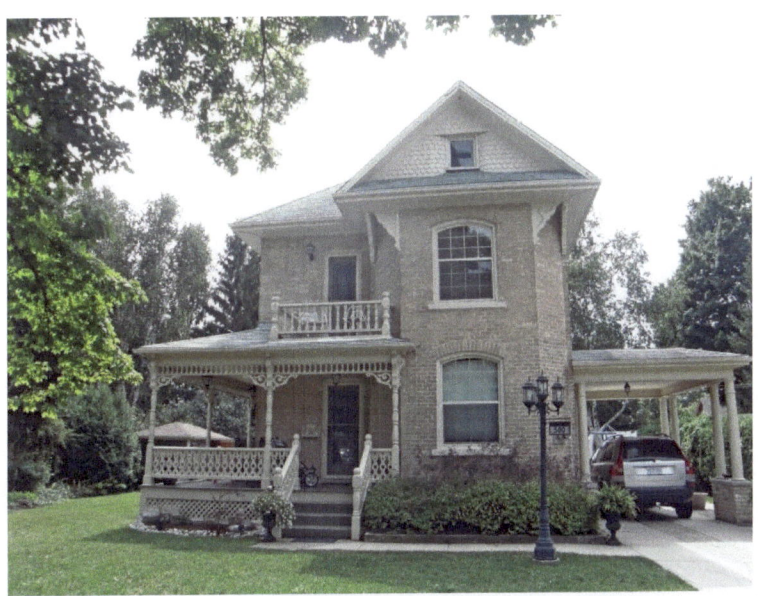

500 Green Street - two-and-a-half storey tower-like bay with projecting eaves and large fretwork pieces resembling brackets, 2nd floor balcony

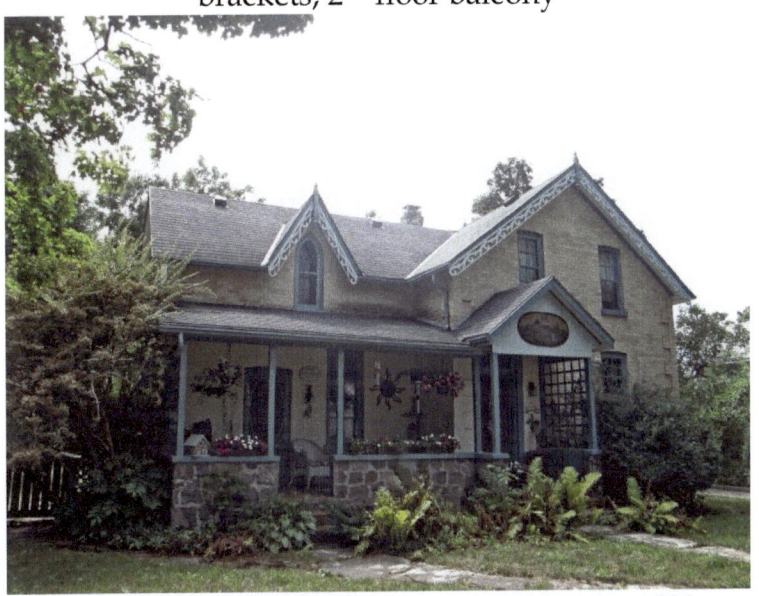

464 Mill Street – Ezra Swartz, Merchant – 1900
Gothic Revival – Verge board trim, cobblestone verandah

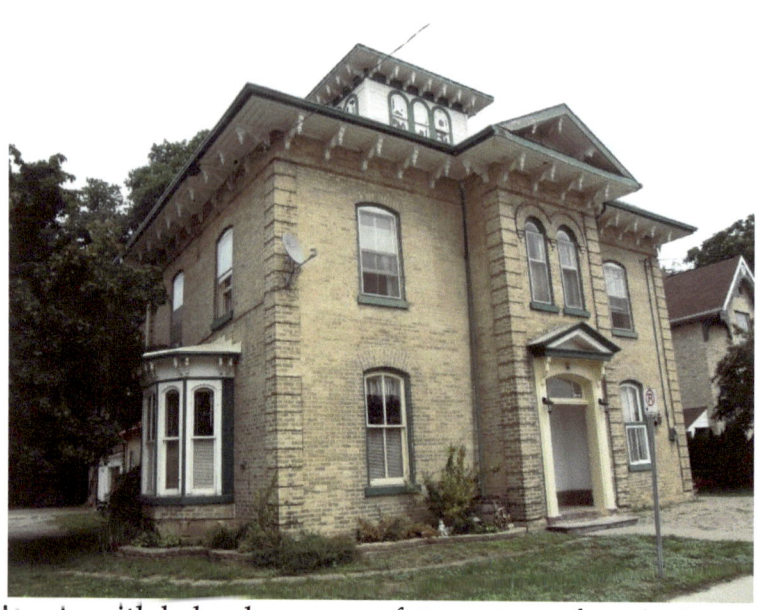

Italianate with belvedere on roof, two storey frontispiece with triangular pediment and arched window hoods, single cornice brackets, bay window on side

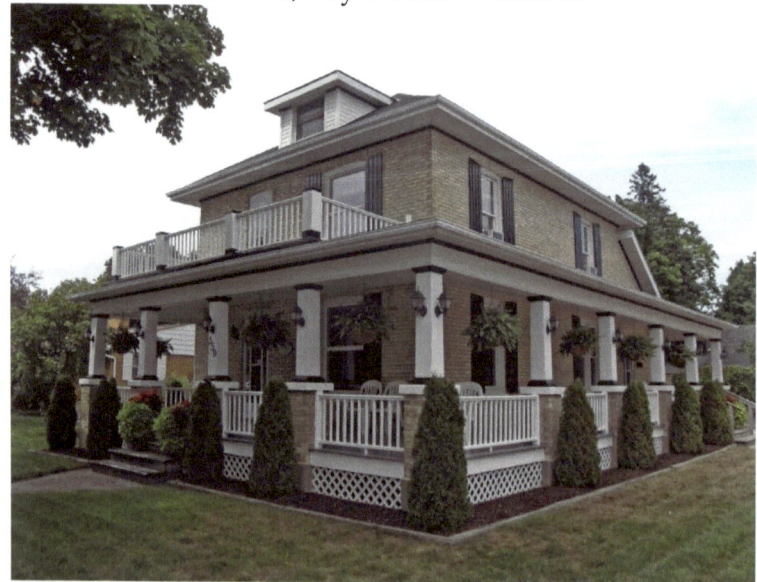

559 Mill Street – Italianate style, wrap-around porch, second floor balcony, dormer in attic – Henry Ebert, Merchant - 1923

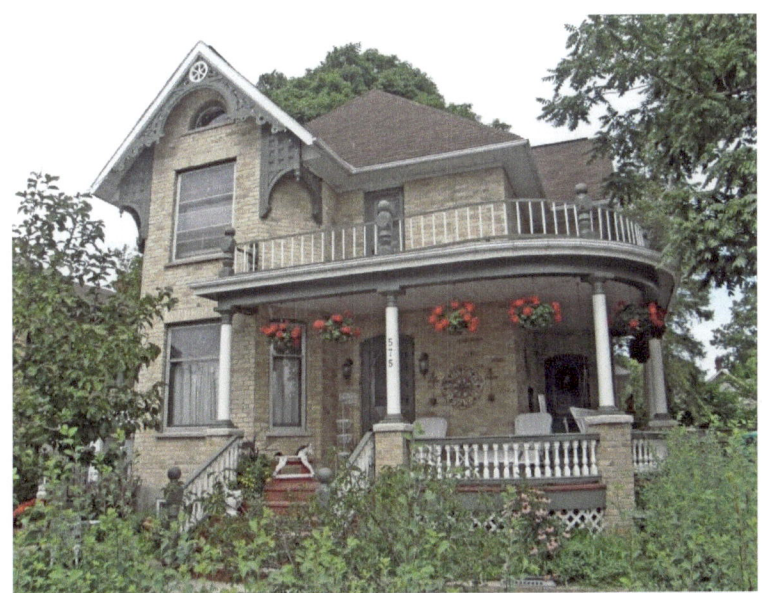

#575 – Italianate style with two-and-a-half storey tower-like bay with projecting eaves and large fretwork pieces resembling brackets, wrap-around verandah on first and second storeys

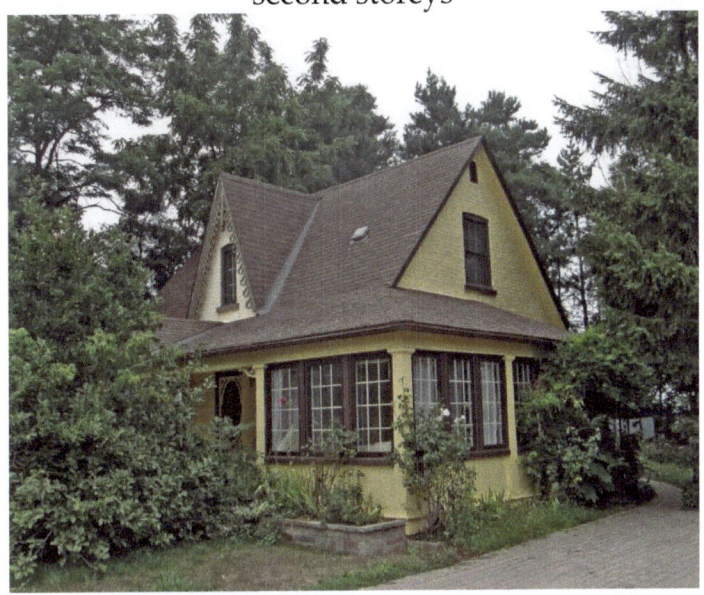

Gothic Cottage – Verge board trim on gable

There are lots more beautiful homes in Port Elgin Book 2. Here is one example.

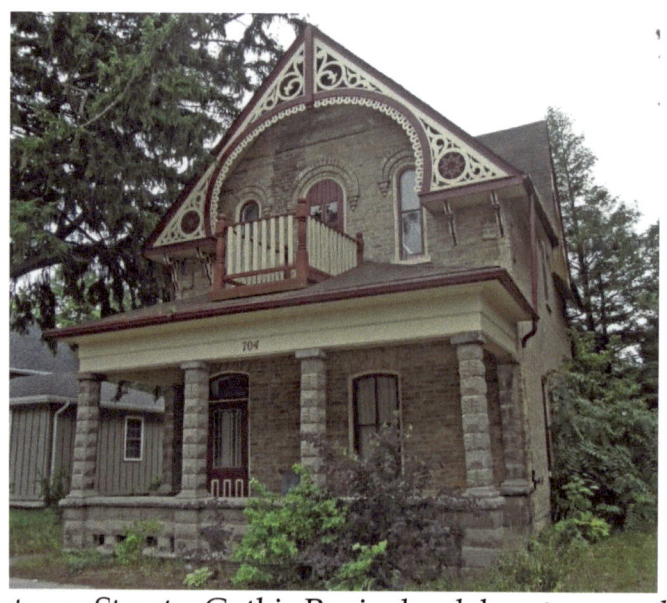

704 Gustavus Street – Gothic Revival – elaborate verge boards, Romanesque style arched window voussoirs – yellow brick – Book 2

Wingham, Ontario – My Top 9 Picks

In the early 1850s, settlers began moving into the townships in the Queen's Bush north of the Huron Tract. One of these townships, Turnberry, was surveyed by 1853 and a plot for a market town was designated where two branches of the Maitland River met. Among the earliest settlers on the plot was John Cornyn who was operating a hotel here in 1861. A year later a post office named Wingham was established and by 1866 Wingham had become a prominent supply and distributing centre for the agricultural and lumbering area. In the 1870s railway expansion stimulated growth and led to Wingham's incorporation as a village in 1874 with a population of 700. Five years later with a population of 2000, Wingham was incorporated as a town.

Wingham, located in Huron County at the intersection of County Roads 4 & 86, became part of North Huron municipality in 2001 when the former township of East Wawanosh, the village of Blyth, and the town of Wingham were amalgamated. County Road 86 connects to Kitchener-Waterloo to the east. The main thoroughfare is County Road 4, called Josephine Street within Wingham, which connects to London, Ontario to the south.

Wingham has manufacturing businesses and a variety of retail and service businesses. Wescast Industries has three manufacturing facilities producing auto parts. BI-AX International produces plastic film for use in food packaging and industry. Royal Homes is a manufacturer of pre-fabricated homes. Britespan Building Systems Inc. is a manufacturer of fabric covered steel structure buildings.

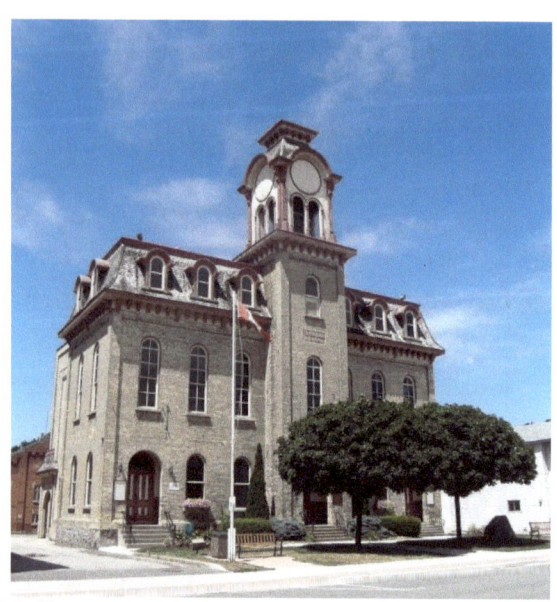

Town Hall A.D. 1890 - mansard roof, dormers, cornice brackets

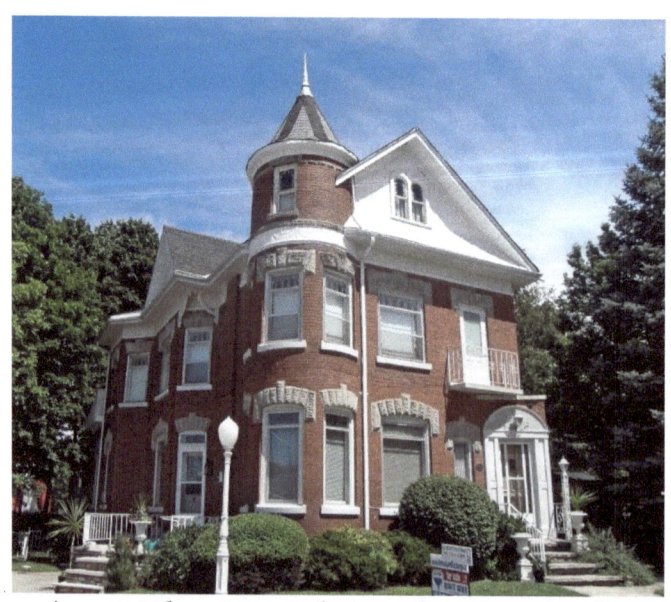

Queen Anne style – turret, fretwork, voussoirs, keystones

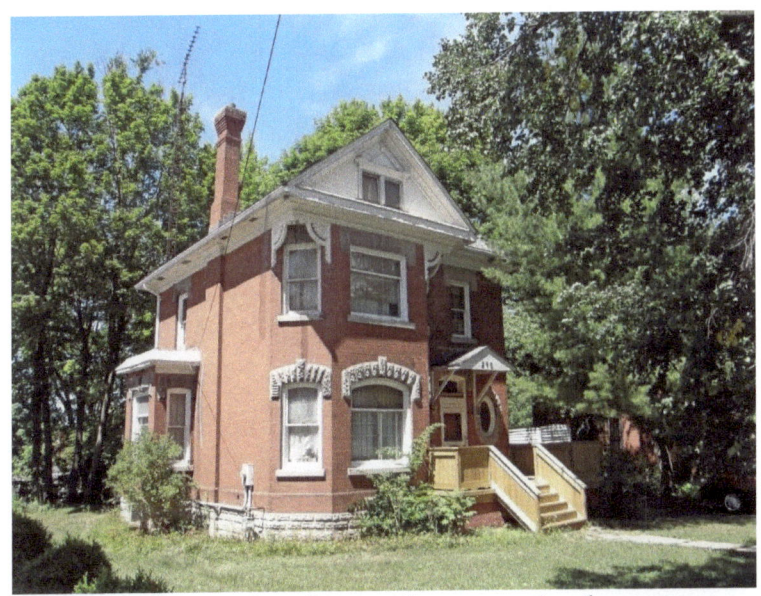

Edwardian style – fretwork, voussoirs, keystones

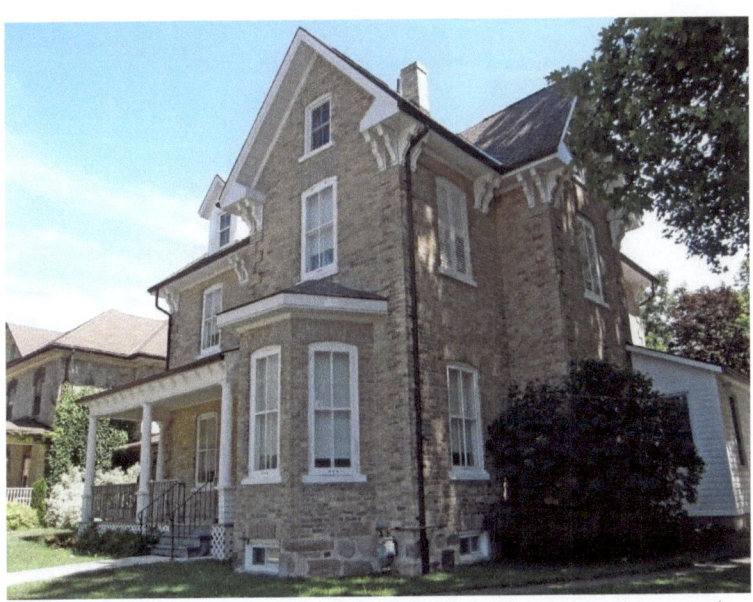

#251 - Gothic Revival, dormers, cornice return, cornice brackets

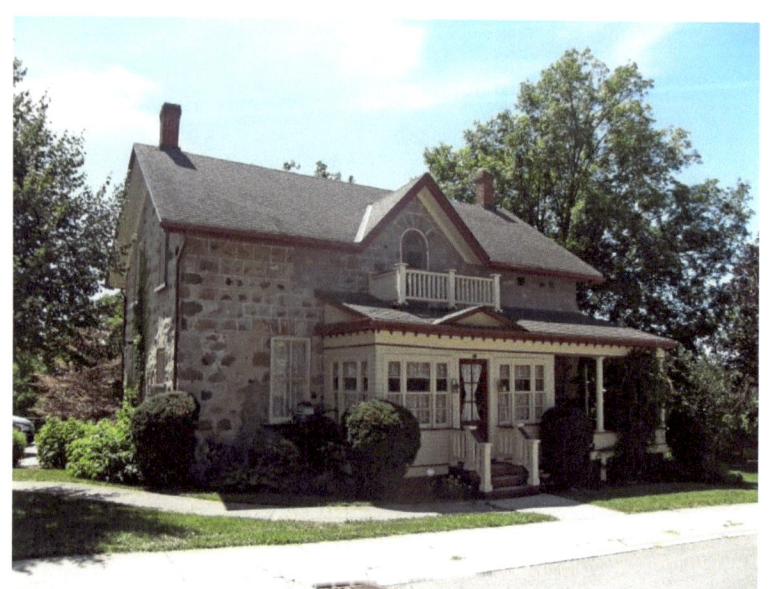

26 John Street East – stone architecture, balcony on second floor

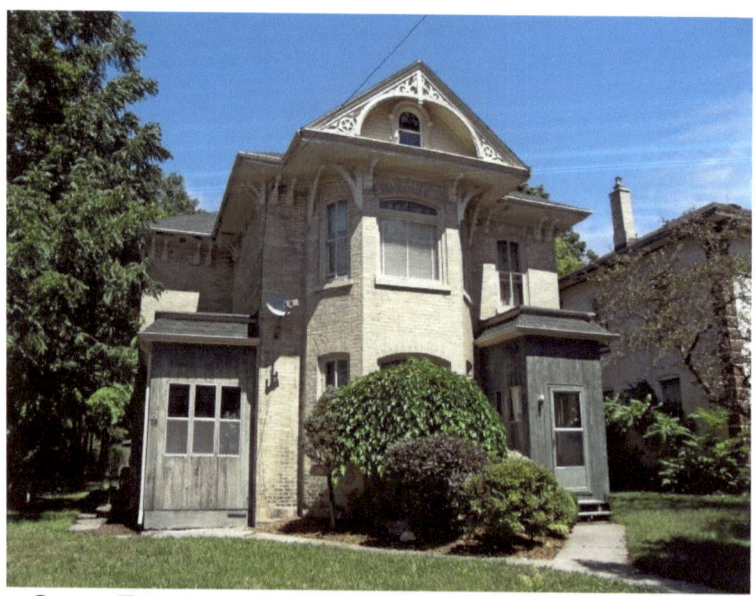

John Street East - verge board trim on gable, cornice brackets under eaves

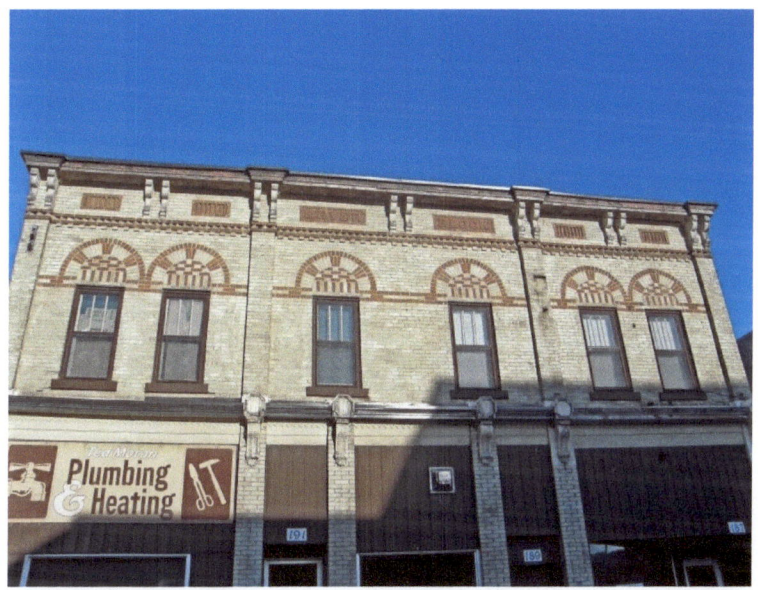

Meyer Block - dichromatic brickwork, cornice brackets

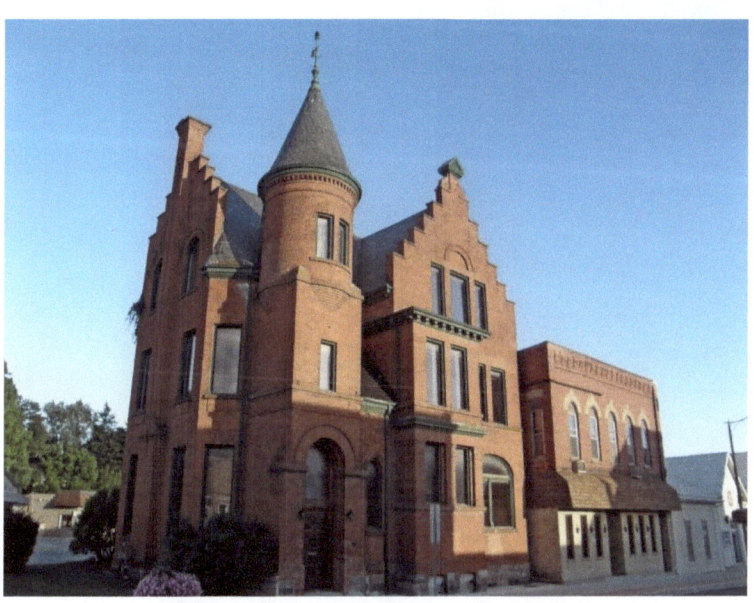

#221 – Queen Anne style, turret

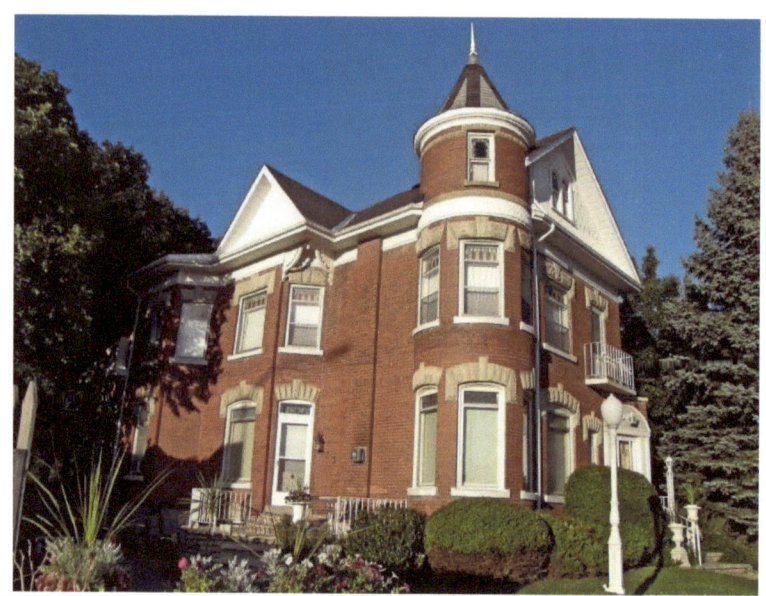

#13 - Queen Anne style, turret, voussoirs, keystones, fretwork

Lucknow, Ontario – My Top 5 Picks

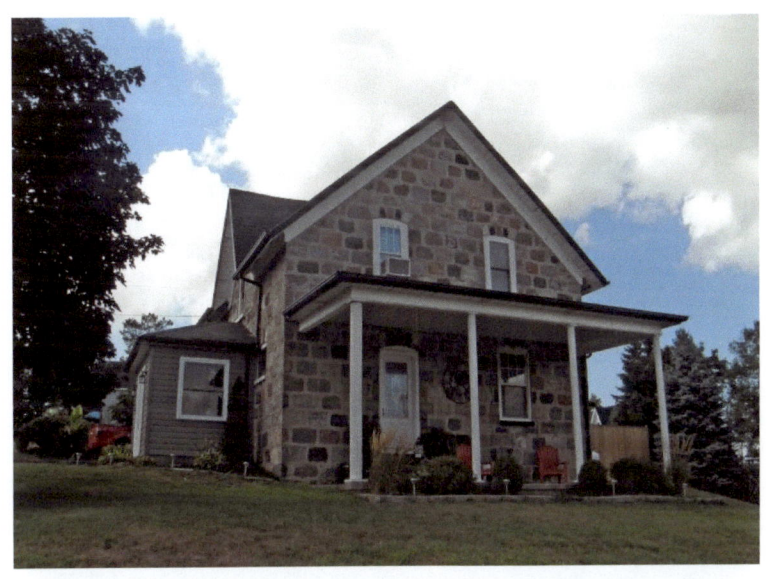

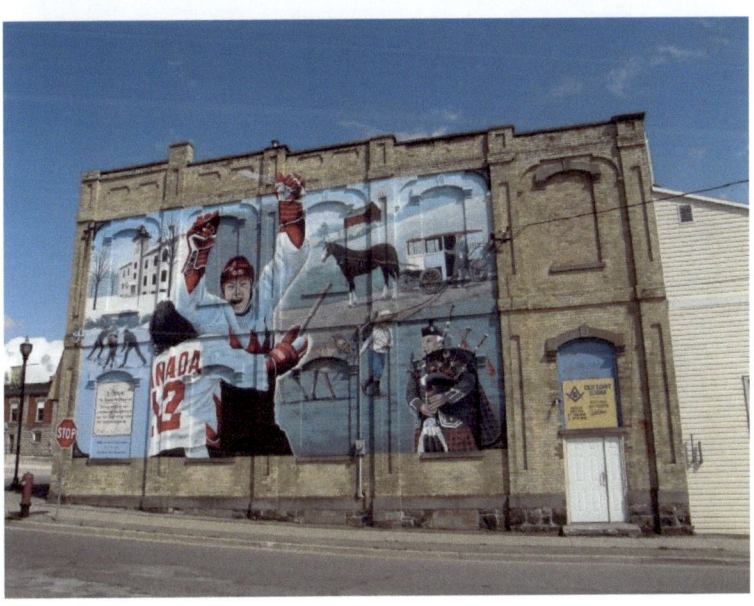

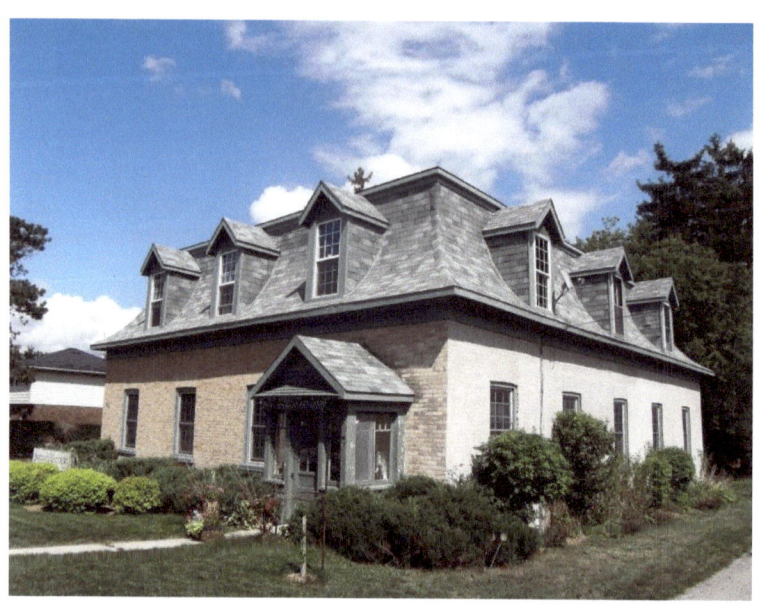

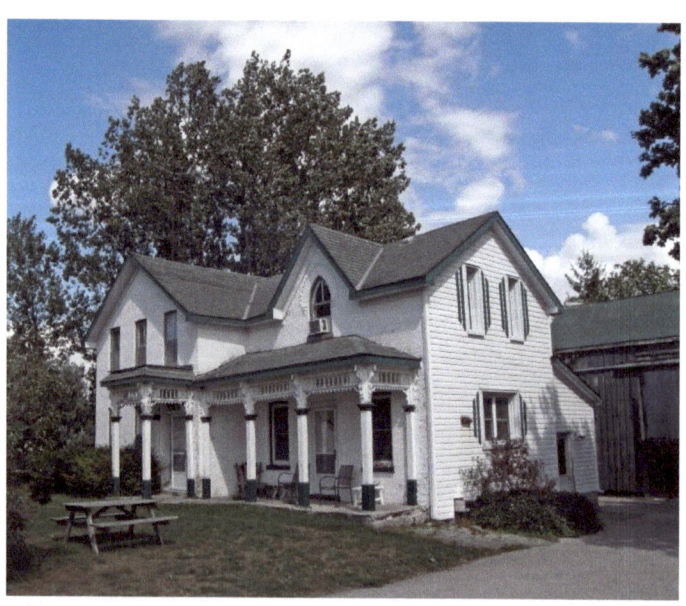

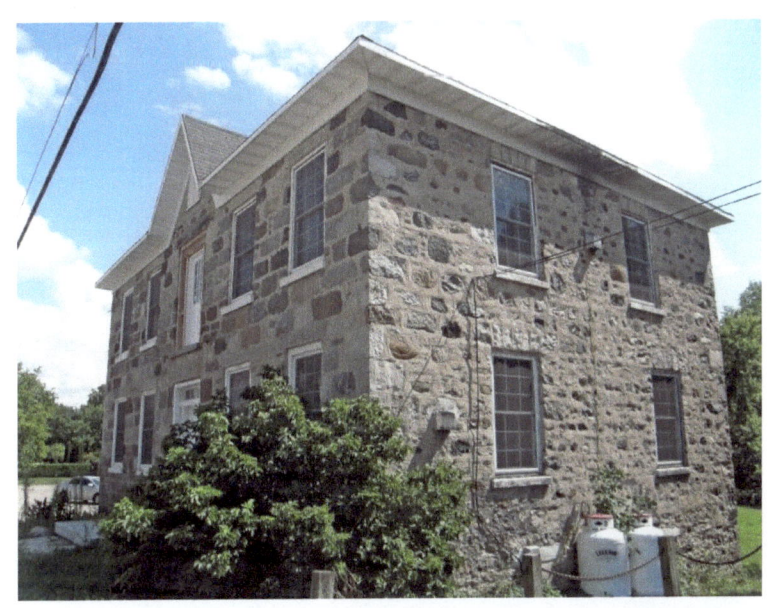

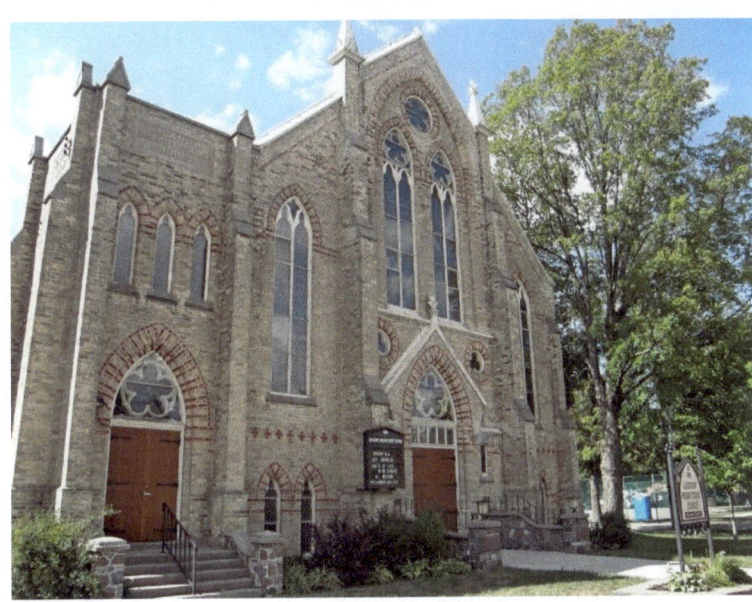

Conestogo, Bloomingdale and West Montrose, Ontario – My Top 12 Picks

The Township of Woolwich is located to the north and east of the City of Waterloo. Woolwich Township began to be settled in the late 1700s, with William Wallace being one of the first settlers arriving in 1798. The township was named in honour of a government surveyor. Woolwich consists of an extensive rural area along with residential communities and industrial/commercial areas. The residential communities include: Elmira, St. Jacobs, Breslau, Conestogo, Heidelberg, Maryhill, Bloomingdale, West Montrose, Foradale, Winterbourne, Crowsfoot Corners, Mundil, Weber, Shanz Station, Martin Grove Village and Eldale.

Connestogo is located at the junction of the Grand and Conestogo Rivers in the township of Woolwich in Waterloo Region. The area was first settled in the 1820s by predominantly Mennonite settlers who had emigrated from Pennsylvania. They were followed by people of German and British background.

The first mill in Woolwich Township was built in Conestogo in 1844 by David Musselman. Known earlier as Musselman's Mills, the settlement was renamed Conestogo in 1852. The name originated from the town and river of Conestoga in Lancaster County, Pennsylvania.

By the middle of the 19th century, Conestogo was a thriving community of about 300 people. It boasted a number of businesses, including a foundry, flour mill, sawmill, furniture factory, paint factory, flax mill, distillery, four hotels, three blacksmiths, two wagon makers and a cooperage, among others. Two local brickyards produced the bricks of which many Conestogo buildings were constructed. The slow pace of Conestogo's development after the 1870s resulted in much of the architectural heritage being well preserved.

The feed mill closed its feed production operation in 2008. New retail stores such as the Conestogo Mercantile and Baby Charlotte do business alongside the antique store and the well-known restaurant and dinner theatre, the Blackforest Inn.

Bloomingdale was named in 1861, likely by a settler from Pennsylvania after Bloomingdale in Luzerne County, Pennsylvania.

West Montrose straddles the Grand River, one of Canada's historic rivers. West Montrose was settled in 1806 by Scots from Montrose, Scotland. The village was an industrious community with a woolen mill, saw mill, lime kiln, feed mill, two blacksmith shops, shoemaker and several stores. In 1902 the railway built tracks and a station north of the village to transport goods and livestock. Today the peaceful village is surrounded by Mennonite farms and most of the people living in the community commute to larger centers to work. The more recent outlying town is home to many large residences.

The West Montrose covered bridge was constructed in 1881 by John and Benjamin Bear and is best known for being the last remaining historical covered bridge in Ontario. These bridges were known colloquially as 'kissing bridges' since couples would be out of sight as they passed through the bridge. While the original bridge was constructed entirely of wood, in a series of repairs and restorations the bridge uses a combination of materials but retains its original form.

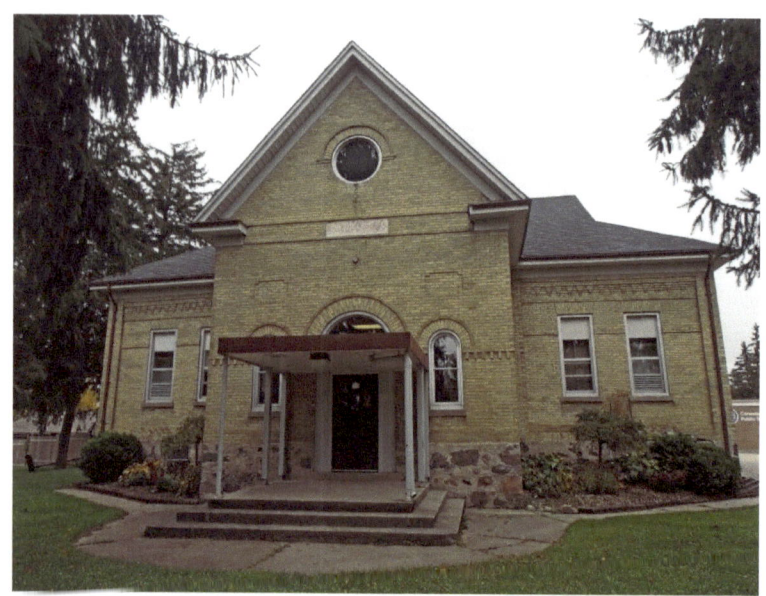

Conestogo Public School – Gothic, Romanesque-style central window arches, beveled dentil molding on side sections

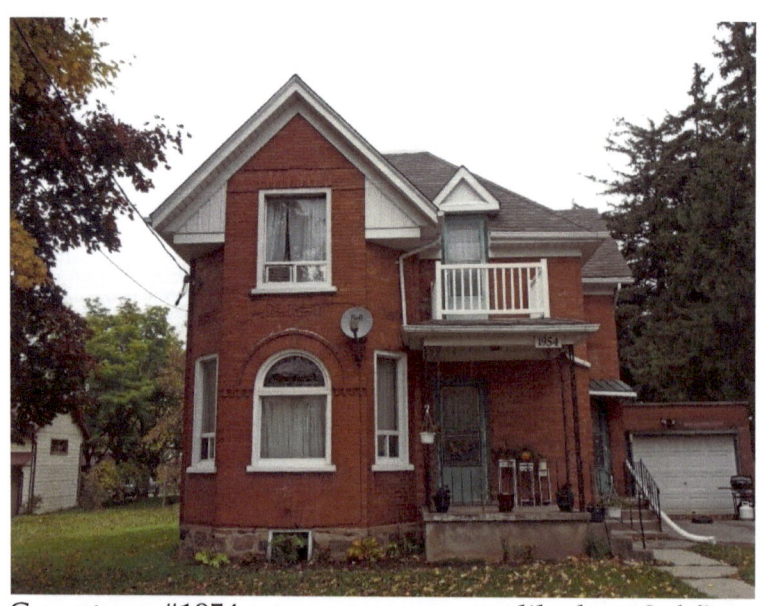

Conestogo #1954 – two-storey tower-like bay, 2nd floor balcony

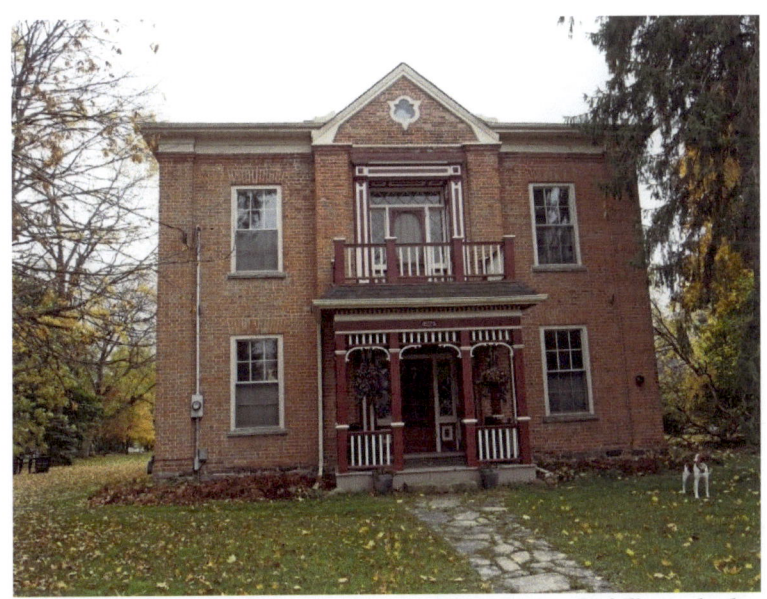

1939 Sawmill Road, Conestogo - Italianate – 2nd floor balcony, both 1st and 2nd floor entrances

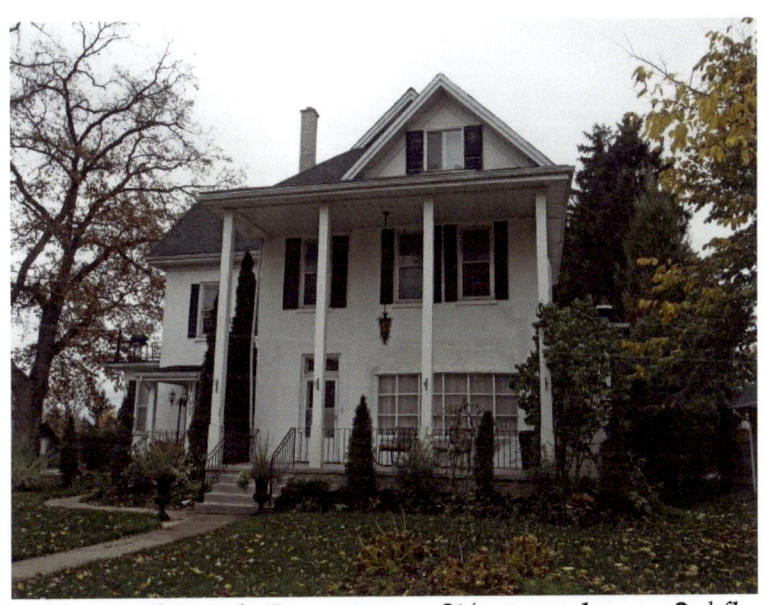

1907 Sawmill Road, Conestogo – 2½ storey home, 2nd floor side balcony

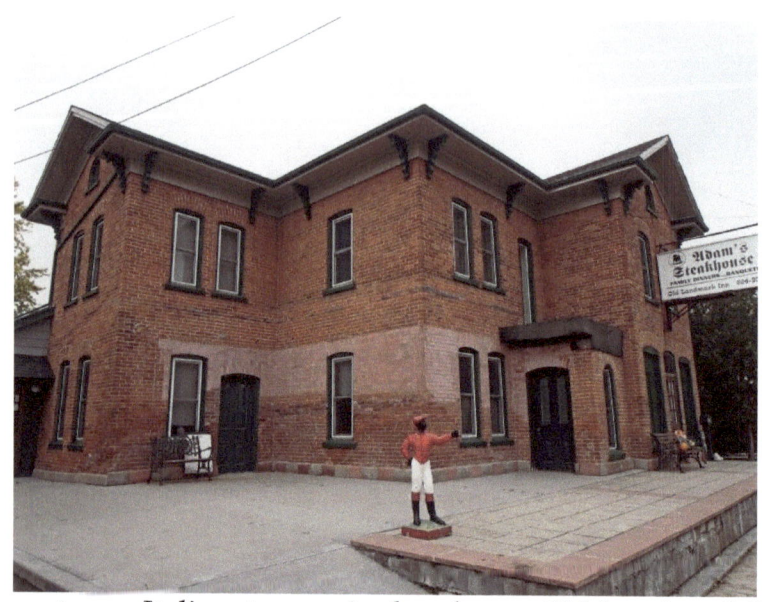

Conestogo - Italianate, cornice brackets – Old Landmark Inn

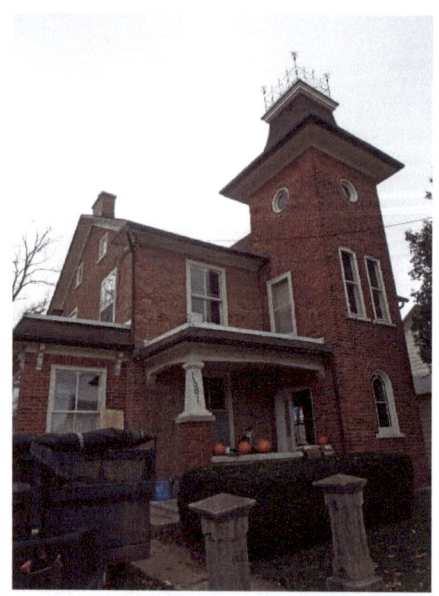

1861 Sawmill Road, Conestogo - 3 storey tower with widow's walk and iron cresting, cornice brackets

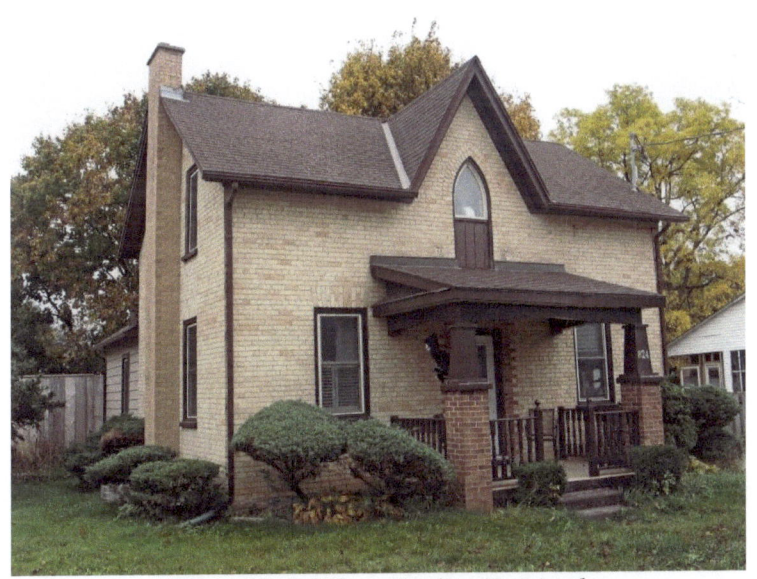

Bloomingdale - Gothic Revival

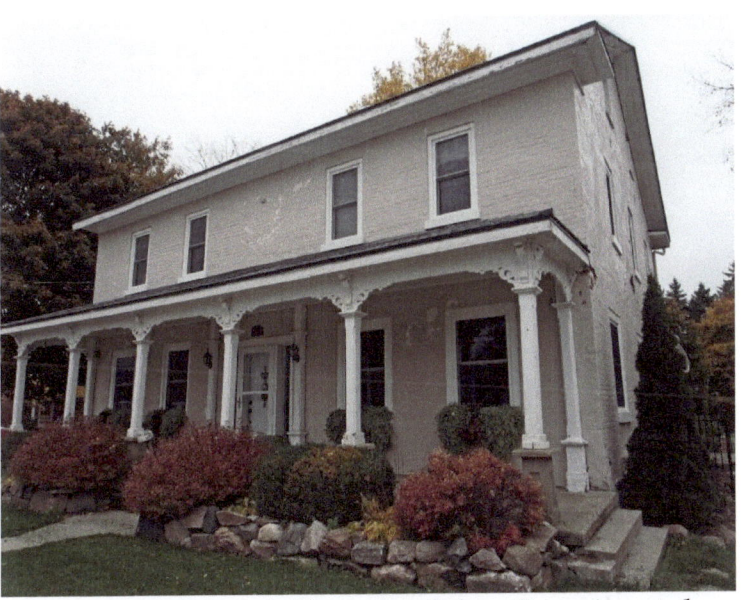

812 Sawmill Road, Bloomingdale – Georgian style

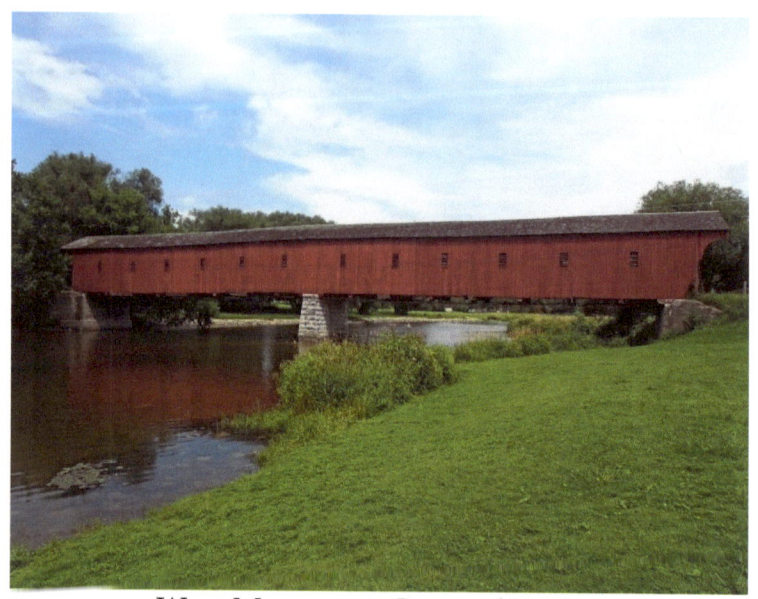

West Montrose - Covered Bridge

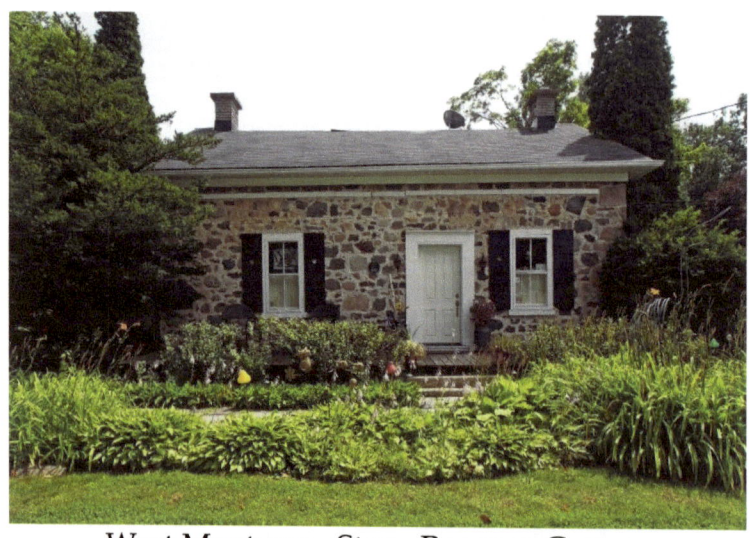

West Montrose - Stone Regency Cottage

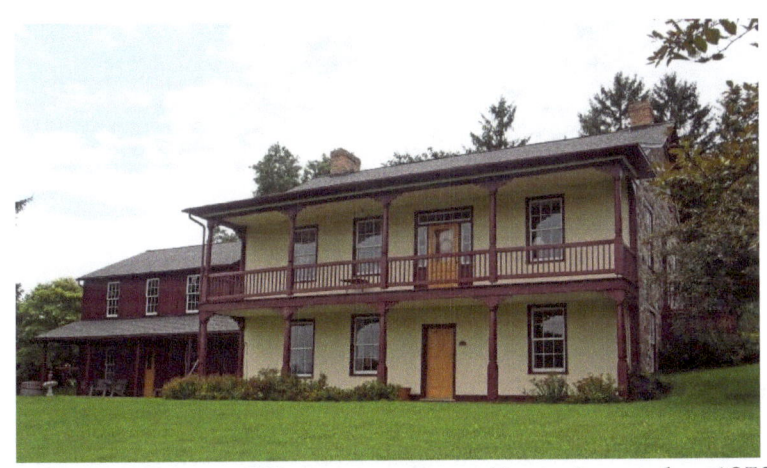

West Montrose - #52 - two storeys, Georgian style - 1858
Heritage Building
With end wall of stone

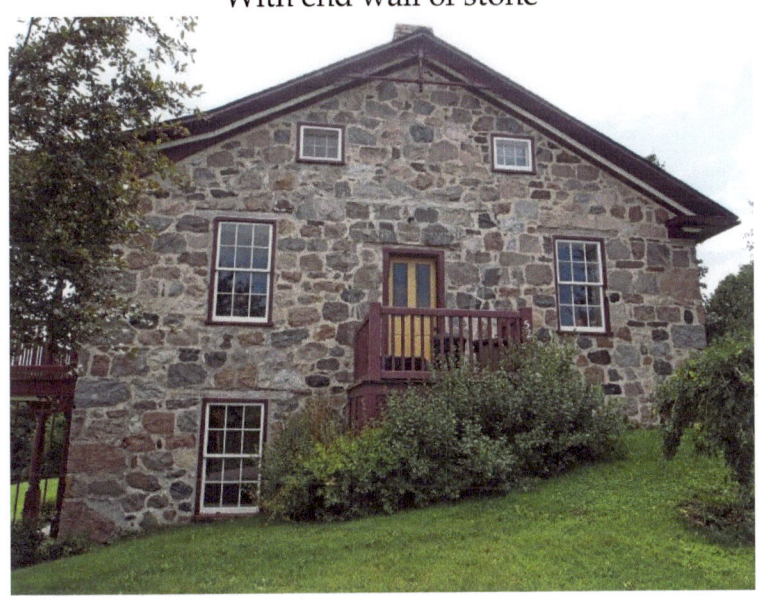

Delhi, Ontario – My Top 5 Picks

Norfolk County is a rural municipality on the north shore of Lake Erie in Southwestern Ontario. The county seat and largest community is Simcoe. Some of the most notable communities in Norfolk County are Delhi, Port Dover, Simcoe, and Waterford.

Surrounding its many small communities is some of the most fertile land in Ontario. With a mild climate and lengthy growing season, the region has long been the centre of the Ontario tobacco belt. Many farmers have begun the process of diversifying their crop selections to include lavender, ginseng, hazelnuts, and wolfberries as tobacco consumption continues to decrease.

Delhi is located off the junction of Highways 53 and 3. Founded by Frederick Sovereign as Sovereign's Corners around 1826, the community was renamed Fredericksburg and eventually its present-day name of Delhi, the name usually attributed locally to a postmaster honoring a major city of the British Empire, Delhi, India. Prior to 1880, this town was known for its lumber industry.

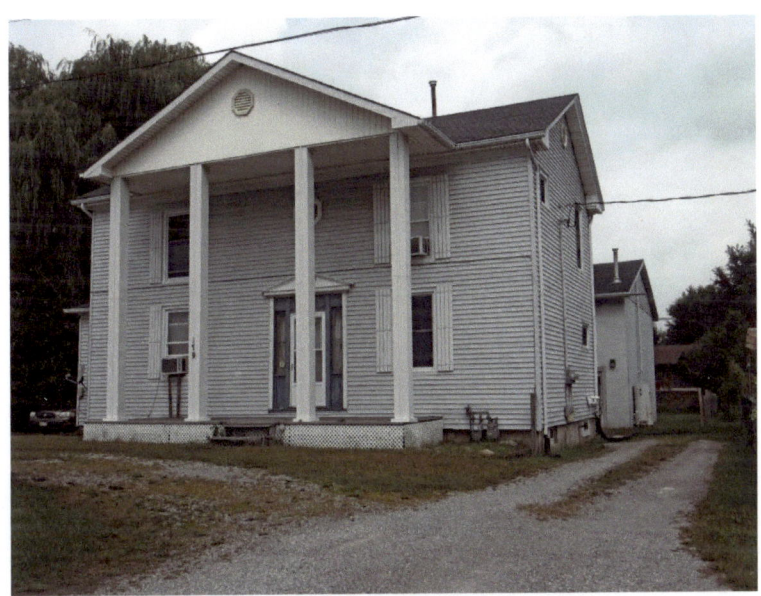

Classical Greek

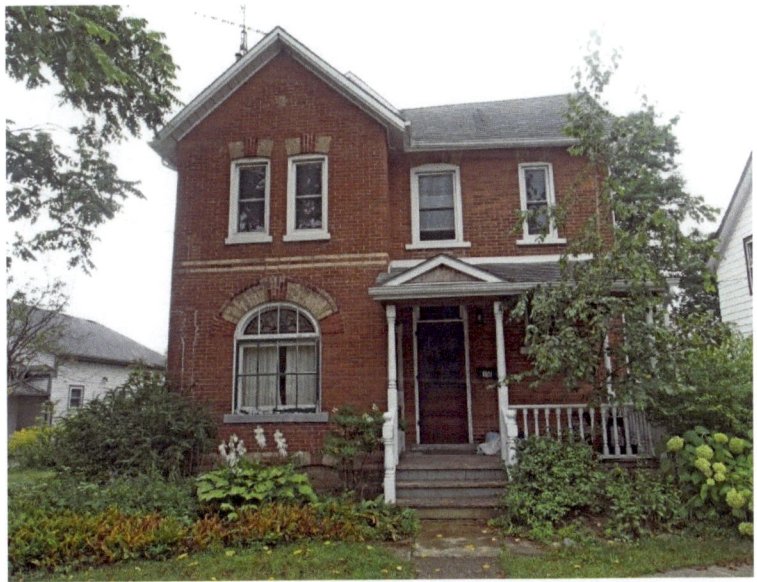

Gothic Revival, banding, dichromatic brickwork, pediment

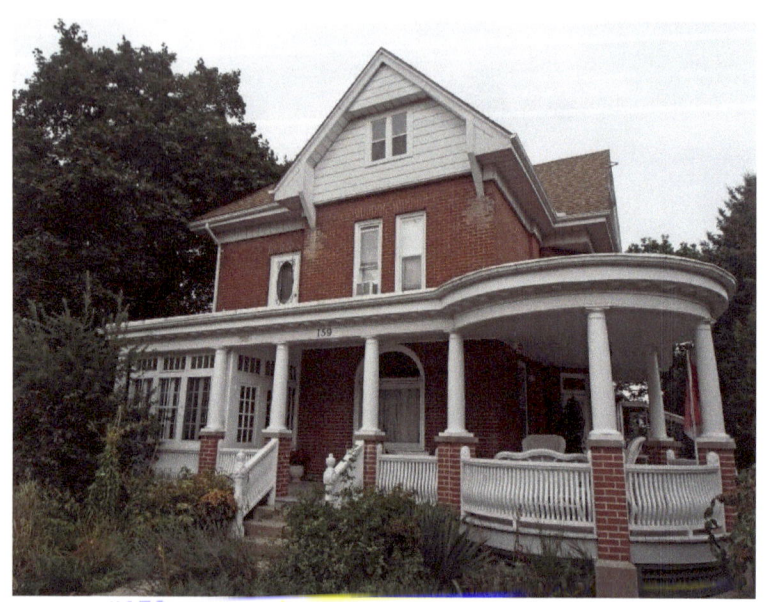

#159 - Victorian – wraparound verandah

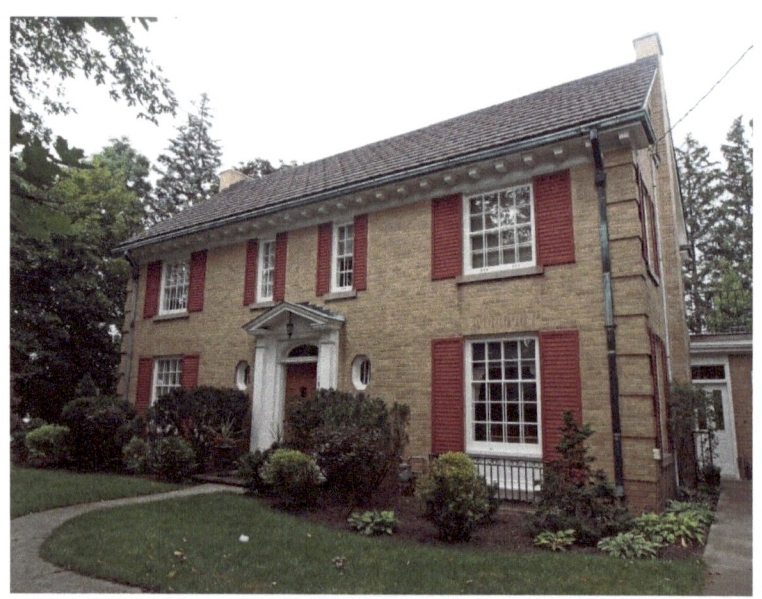

#187 – Georgian – fanlight (transom window) above door

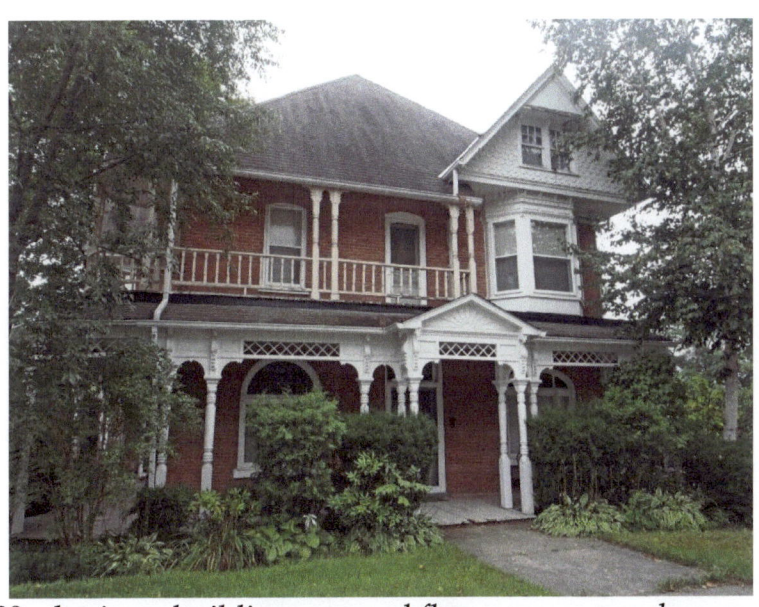

#180 – heritage building - second floor wraparound verandah with cone-shaped roof with turned spindles, fretwork, dormer, bay window

Waterford, Ontario – My Top 8 Picks

Waterford is located on Pleasant Ridge Road, or old Highway 24 in Norfolk County, south of Brantford, north of Simcoe and southwest of Ohsweken. Waterford was established in 1794 with saw and grist mills on Nanticoke Creek. An early major industry was the agricultural implement factory built by James Green, a local merchant. The area surrounding the town is primarily agricultural land with tomatoes, tobacco and corn among the main crops. With the decline of the tobacco industry, area farmers have suffered, but ginseng is being grown on some farms. In 1979 a freak tornado swept through the town, knocked down trees, and damaged houses and public property.

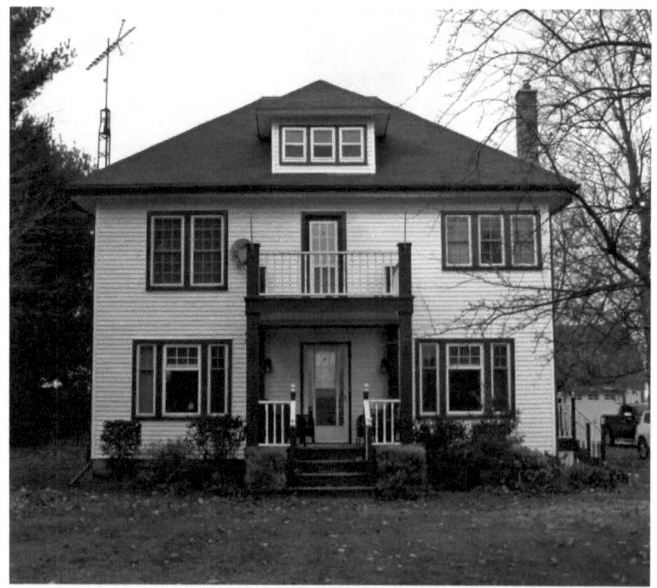

Italianate, hipped roof, dormer, second floor balcony

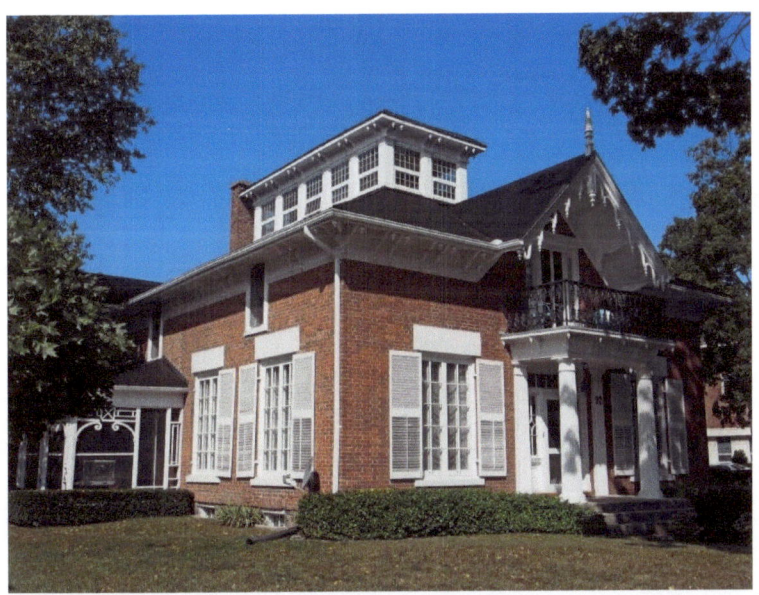

92 Main Street – Italianate, belvedere on roof, paired cornice brackets, verge board and finial on gables, second floor balcony, Doric columns

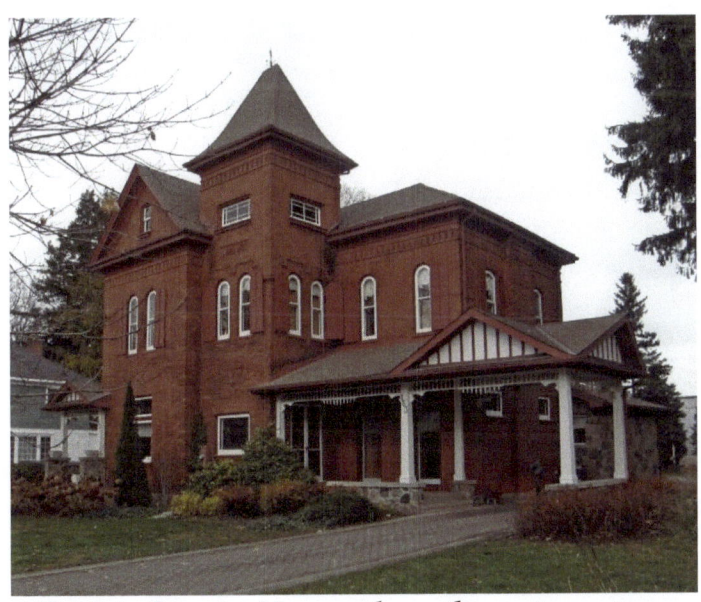

163 Main Street – Vernacular – three storey tower

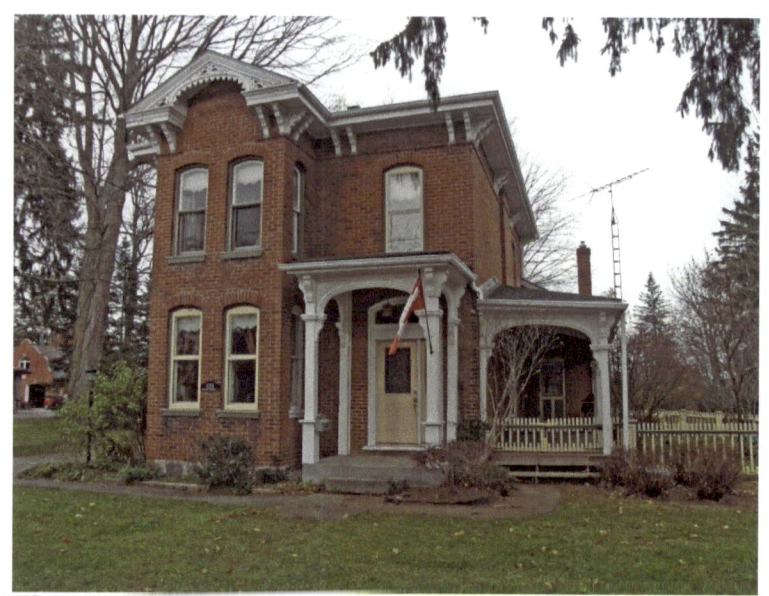

173 Main Street – two-storey tower-like bay capped with bargeboard trim on gable

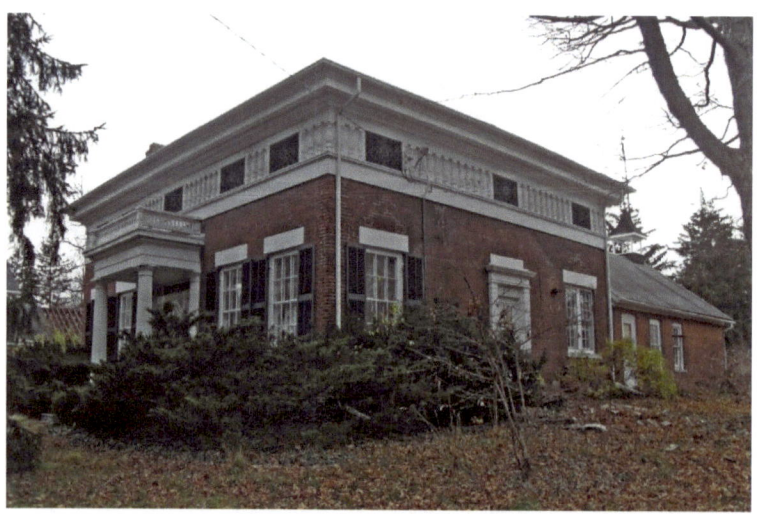

Italianate - Doric pillars

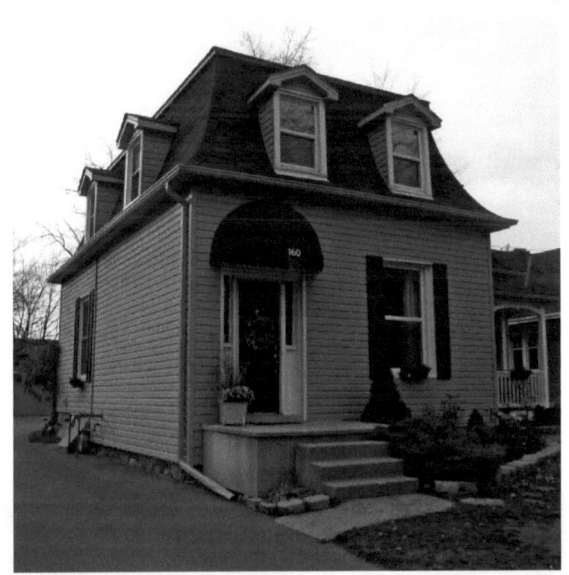

160 Main Street – Second Empire style, mansard roof, dormers

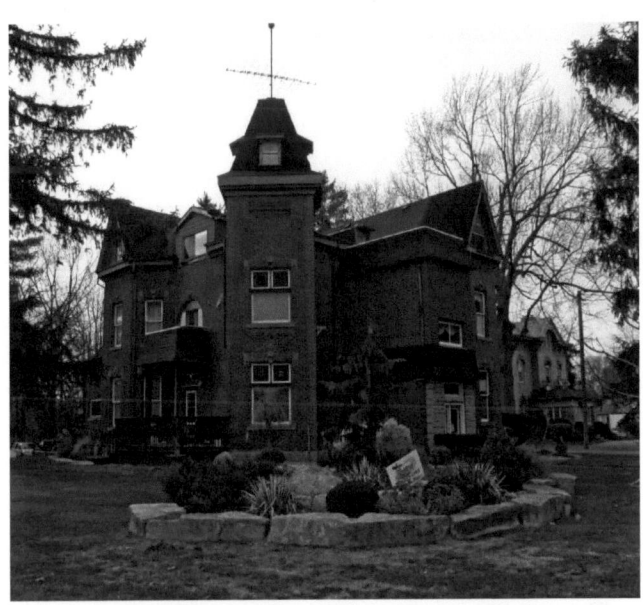

Queen Anne – 3½ storey tower

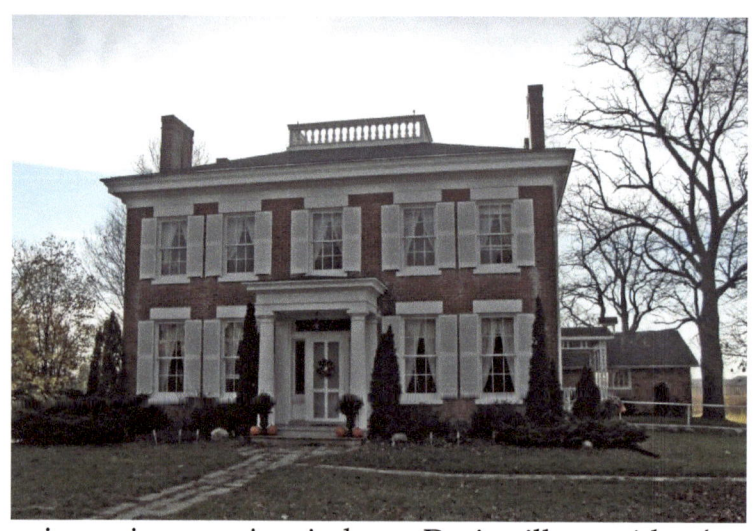

Georgian – six-over-six windows, Doric pillars, widow's walk on rooftop, sidelights and transom window around door

Waterloo, Ontario – My Top 12 Picks

Waterloo is a city in Southern Ontario. The Conestogo Parkway and Highway 8 connect Waterloo with Kitchener, Cambridge, Highway 7/8, and Highway 401. Waterloo shares several of its north-south arterial roads with neighboring Kitchener.

Waterloo was built on land that was part of a parcel of 675,000 acres assigned in 1784 to the Iroquois alliance that made up the League of Six Nations. Almost immediately, the native groups began to sell some of the land. Between 1796 and 1798, 93,000 acres were sold through a Crown Grant to Richard Beasley, with the Six Nations Indians continuing to hold the mortgage on the lands.

The first immigrants to the area were Mennonites from Pennsylvania. They bought deeds to land parcels from Beasley and began moving into the area in 1804. The following year, a group of twenty-six Mennonites pooled resources to purchase all of the unsold land from Beasley and discharge the mortgage held by the Six Nations Indians.

The Mennonites divided the land into smaller lots; two lots initially owned by Abraham Erb became the central core of Waterloo. Erb built a sawmill on Beaver, now Laurel, Creek in 1808 and in 1816 built the area's first grist mill which farmers from miles around used to grind their wheat into flour, a very important staple.

In 1816, the new township was named after Waterloo, Belgium, the site of the Battle of Waterloo, which had ended the Napoleonic Wars in Europe. After that war, the area became a popular destination for German immigrants. By the 1840s, German settlers were the dominant segment of the population. Many Germans settled in the small hamlet to the southeast of Waterloo. In their honour, the village was named Berlin in 1833 (renamed to Kitchener in 1916). Berlin was chosen as the site of the seat for the County of Waterloo in 1853.

The inhabitants established Waterloo as an important industrial and commercial centre. The village had a council chamber, fire hall, post office, library, and four steam-powered factories, including the Granite Mills and Distillery which became the Seagram Company.

The Grand River flows southward along the east side of the city. Its most significant tributary within the city is Laurel Creek, whose source lies just to the west of the city limits and its mouth just to the east, and crosses much of the city's central areas including the University of Waterloo lands and Waterloo Park; it flows under the uptown area in a culvert. In the west end of the city, the Waterloo Moraine provides over 300,000 people in the region with drinking water. Much of the gently hilly Waterloo Moraine underlies existing developed areas.

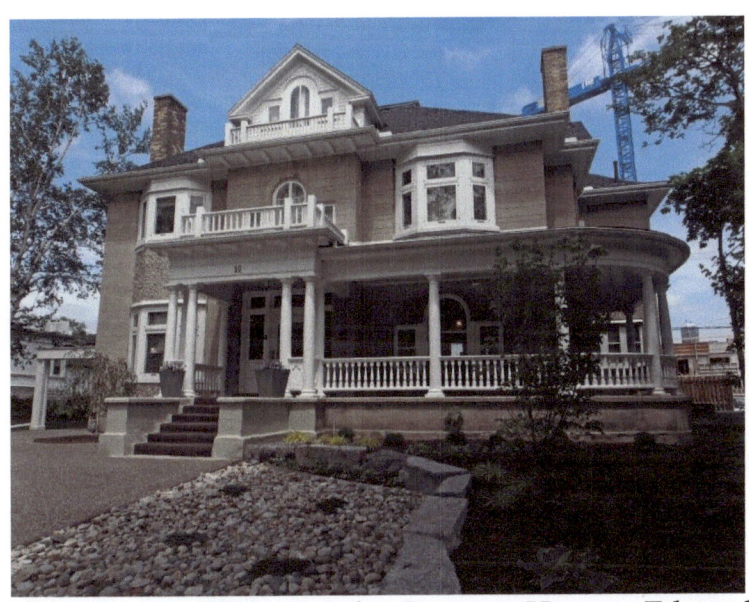

50 Albert Street – 1903 – Snyder-Seagram House – Edwardian Classical in parged concrete – superposed sets of Palladian windows and bay windows projecting over both storeys; curved, wraparound verandah with classical columns – Book 1

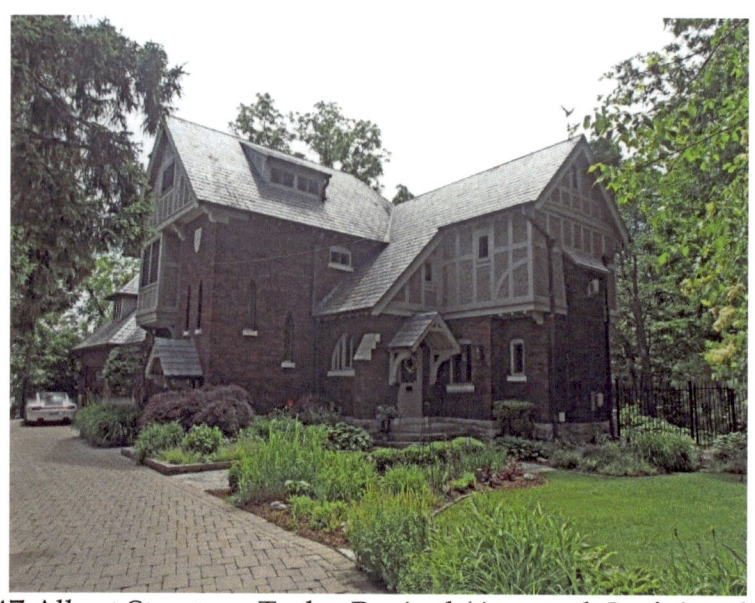

47 Albert Street – a Tudor Revival (Arts and Crafts) style house built in 1924 by the manager of the Globe Furniture Company, a world leader in furniture manufacturing especially church and school furnishings and religious carvings – Book 1

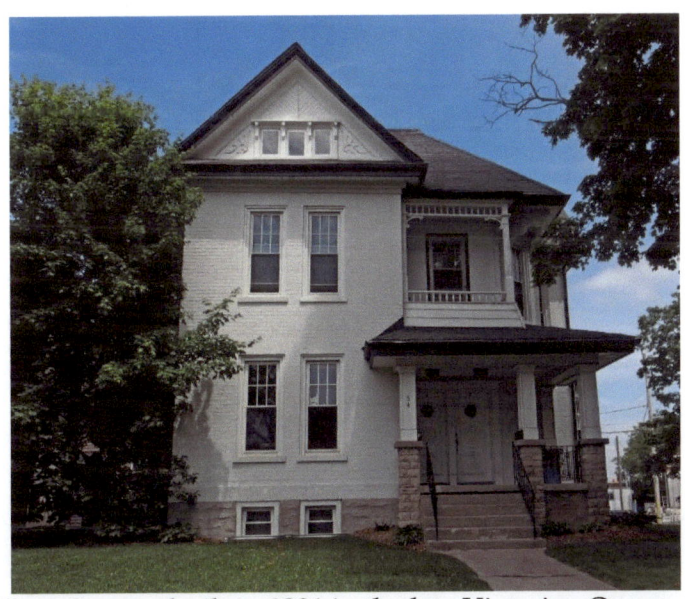

54 Albert Street – built in 1891 in the late Victorian Queen Anne style for Dr. Charles Noecker, the Medical Officer of Health; buff brick walls have been painted – Book 1

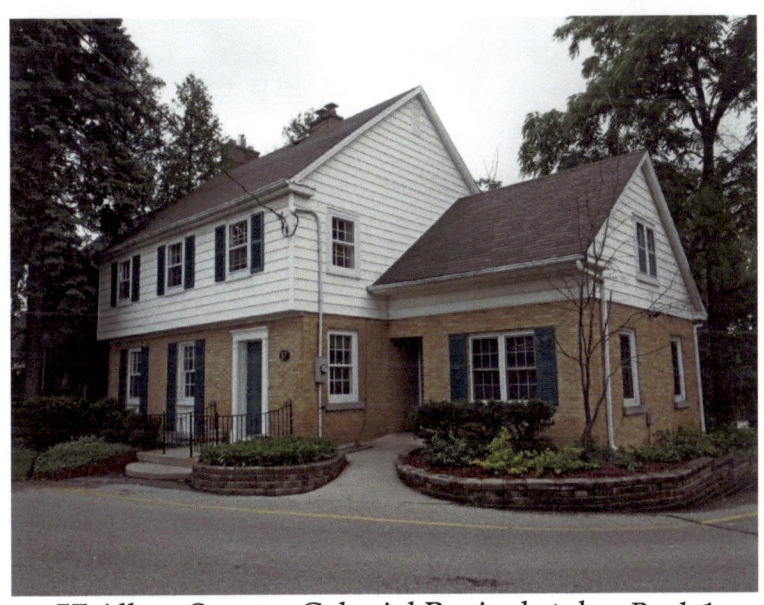

57 Albert Street – Colonial Revival style – Book 1

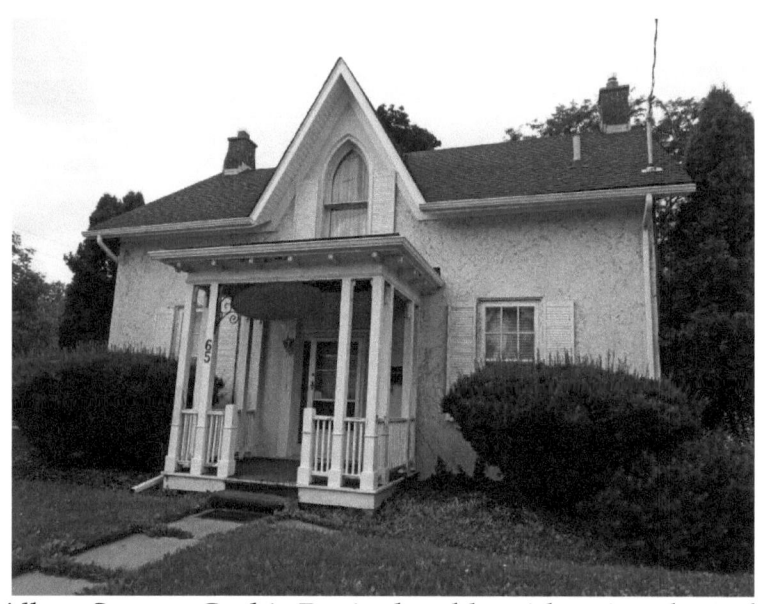

65 Albert Street – Gothic Revival, gable with pointed window, Stucco over brick house built in 1866 by Elias Snider – Book 1

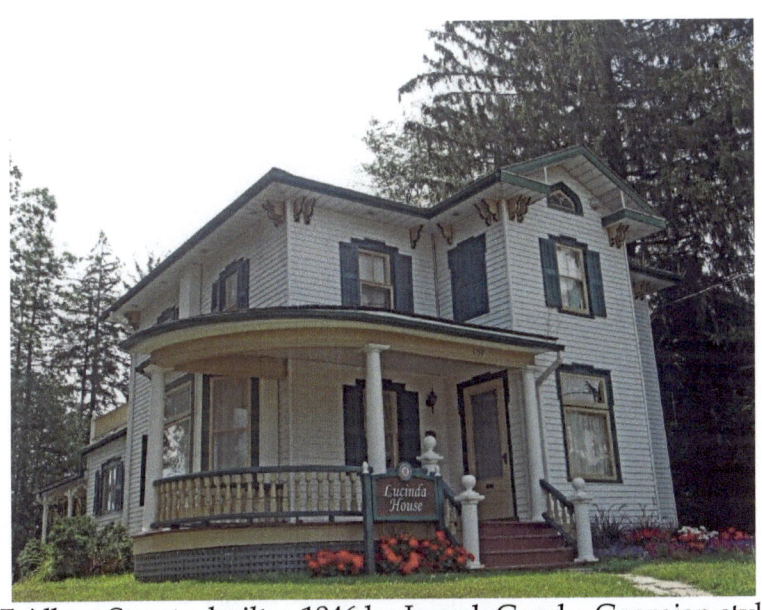

157 Albert Street – built c. 1846 by Joseph Good – Georgian style – molded trim, shutters, eared window pediments, blind attic window, cornice return on front gable; modified by Allan Shantz in 1896 – semi-circular verandah with newel posts topped by cannon ball finials, stained glass parlor window – give late-Victorian appearance – Book 1

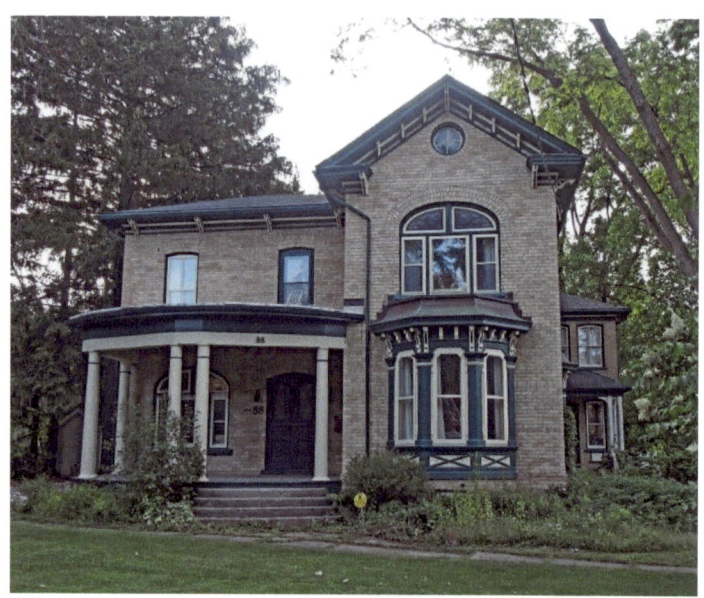

88 William Street West – 1880 – Victorian - 2½ storey projecting rectangular bay, cornice return on gable, bay window with cornice brackets, wraparound verandah, stained glass windows – Book 2

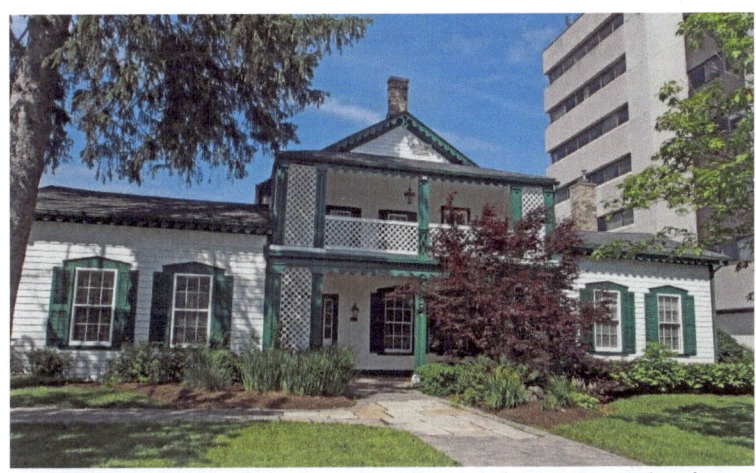

172 King Street South – the original portion, the first homestead in Waterloo, was built about 1812 by Abraham Erb; subsequent additions – white clapboard; wings on either side of center section and second-storey balcony added 1855; 6-over-6 arrangement of window panes is a Georgian characteristic; symmetrical front porch between two wings with latticework, Gothic bargeboard and Doric columns reflects a Regency influence. – Book 2

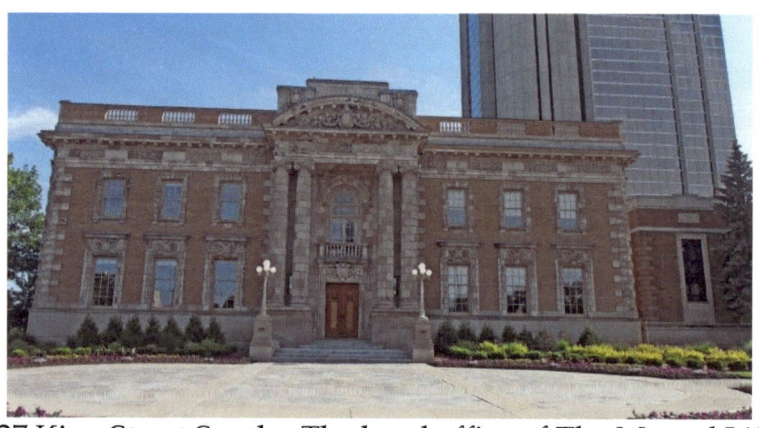

227 King Street South - The head office of The Mutual Life Assurance Company of Canada (now head office of Sun Life Financial's Canadian operations) was completed in 1912. The Renaissance Revival style building is ornamented with features such as the two-storey fluted paired Ionic columns supporting a large segmental arch above the main doors, elaborate window surrounds, and a parapet with a balustrade. It is clad in light brown and yellow Roman brick, and embellished with projecting pedimented bays and quoins. Many of the decorative details on the façade are made from imported English terra cotta. Situated within a Beaux Arts designed landscape, the building is a unique and iconic corporate pavilion. The monumental scale of the building and its rich ornamentation symbolize the importance and stability of Waterloo's first life insurance company and reflect the town's early twentieth century prosperity and sense of civic pride. – Book 2

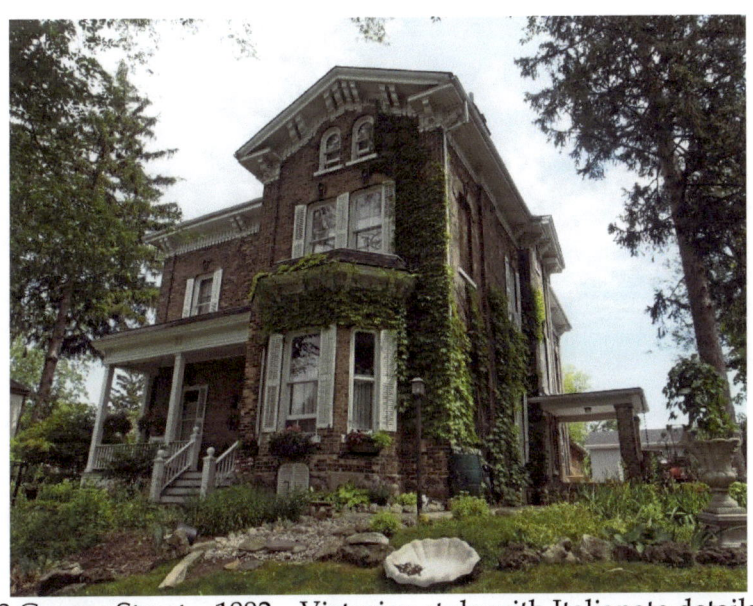

73 George Street – 1882 – Victorian style with Italianate details - fancy brackets under eaves, wood trim below the eaves, bay window; arched windows in the attic of the projecting bay; other windows have rounded corners; double front door; keystones over windows decorated with a motif consisting of a bunch of grapes – Book 2

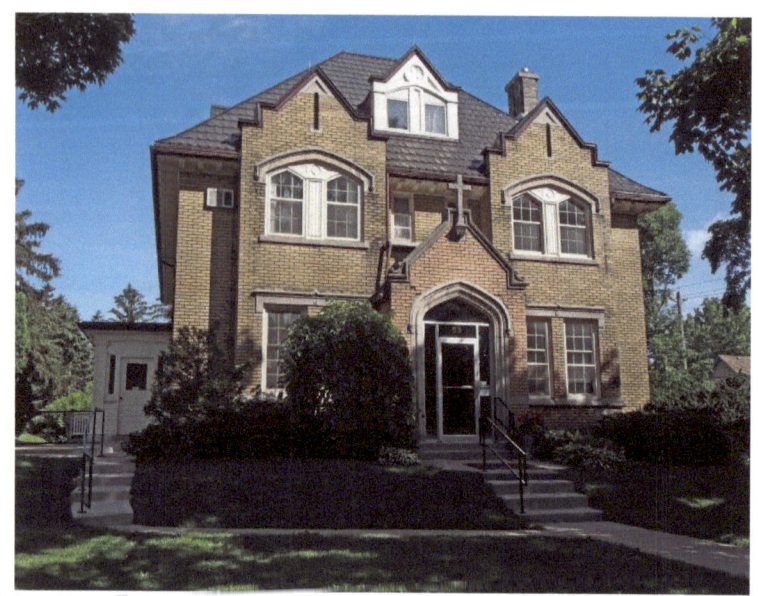

53 Allen Street East – new rectory – 1928 – Period Revival Style – medieval influences – the gables have loopholes, found in medieval architecture as a place for launching arrows – Book 2

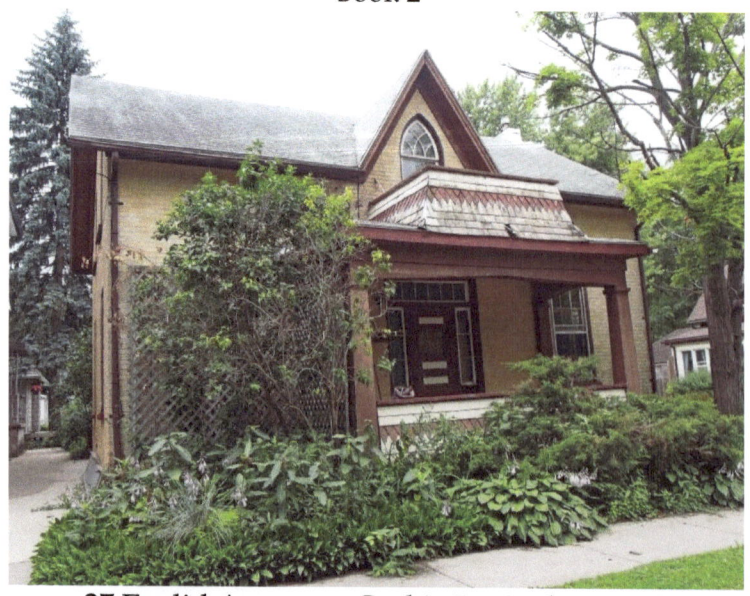

27 Euclid Avenue – Gothic Revival – Book 3

Windsor, Ontario – My Top 13 Picks

Windsor is the southernmost city in Canada. The Detroit River is to the north of the city, which separates it from Detroit, Michigan. Windsor was settled by the French in 1749 as an agricultural settlement. In 1794, after the American Revolution, the settlement of "Sandwich" was founded. It was later renamed Windsor, after the town in Berkshire, England.

Sandwich, Ford City and Walkerville were separate towns until 1935 when they were annexed by Windsor. They remain as historic neighborhoods of Windsor. Walkerville was incorporated as a town in 1890.

The former Town of Walkerville was founded by Hiram Walker in 1858. The New England-born distiller bought two French farms on the south shore of the Detroit River, and the growth of his industry and the town it supported continued for seven decade under his family's guidance.

Railroads played an important part in Walkerville's history. First, the Great Western's extension to Windsor in 1854 opened up opportunities for commercial expansion. Then Walker built his own line in 1885 with government financing, the Lake Erie Essex & Detroit River Railroad, which connected Walkerville with lakeshore towns and farms, and extended as far as St. Thomas. The availability of rail transportation attracted other industrial enterprises to the area, and brought great prosperity to the Walker family and their town.

The Walkerville Land & Building Company was incorporated in 1890 with Hiram's oldest son, Edward Chandler, as president. The Town passed a by-law in 1894 to provide temporary tax exemptions to attract new industries, and to encourage individuals wishing to build homes in Walkerville. Rental properties for the distillery's employees were built. All of the community's amenities were provided by Walker - a fire brigade and police, streetlights, sewers, paved roads and sidewalks, parks, a music hall, a school, library and church.

Walker Road's east side was devoted to industrial manufacturing facilities. Its western edge had modest, brick, semidetached houses; Monmouth Road's semis and terraces replaced rows of cottages, and employees were originally required to rent from the distillery. Argyle Road had a mix of terraces and vernacular houses for a higher rank of employee. Devonshire Road became the main street, with Romanesque Revival semis for management and the clergy. Later, distinctive houses of various architectural styles, popular in the protracted Edwardian Period (1900 to the 1930s), rose on the street, and spilled over onto Kildare Road. The concept was fully realized with the landscaped "island" developed as the site of St. Mary's Anglican Church - the sons' memorial to their parents, and the erection of Willistead Manor on the former Country Club and park lands.

The Arts and Crafts Movement, a philosophy of design founded in England about 1850, emphasized handmade architecture in an age when factory mass-production was taking hold. Every home Albert Kahn designed shows Arts and Crafts influence. Kahn believed that historic period styles were best suited to homes and public institutions, while factories should be utilitarian, brightly illuminated and devoid of ornament.

Hiram Walker was born in East Douglas, Massachusetts, and moved to Detroit in 1838. In 1847 at the age of 30, he married Mary Abigail Williams and they had 7 children, two daughters, Julia Elizabeth and Jennie Melissa, and five sons, Willis Ephraim, Edward Chandler, Franklin Hiram, Alfred (infant), and James Harrington. Edward Chandler, his second son, commissioned the development of Willistead Manor.

He was an American entrepreneur and he purchased 460 acres of land across the Detroit River in the town of Sandwich, near Windsor, Ontario, Canada. In 1858 the flour mill and distillery were completed. The flour produced in his mill benefited the County of Essex's farming community with farmers from all around using the mill.

Mid-summer in 1858 marked the opening of Hiram Walker's whisky operation. The same process which he had used in Detroit was now used in Windsor to distill his alcohol. Spirits were leached through charcoal, a process widely used at the time. Walker began selling his whisky as Hiram Walker's Club Whisky and it became very popular. His Canadian industries quickly took precedent over that of his grain business still located in Detroit. As a result, Hiram Walker travelled by ferry to Canada from his home in Detroit on a daily basis. The trip was a lengthy process as the ferry that brought him to Canada dropped him off in Windsor, which left a long ride by horse and buggy to his flour mill and distillery. Throughout his life, Hiram Walker remained an American citizen but in March 1859 Hiram Walker moved to Canada in order to save time traveling to and from his Canadian businesses.

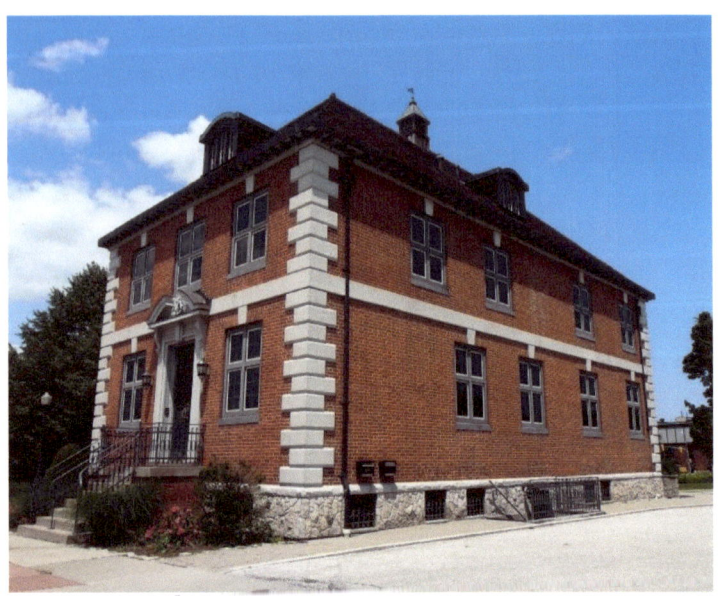

350 Devonshire Road - Walkerville Town Hall - 1904
Classical Revival – symmetrical, belt courses (a continuous row of stones set in the wall), angled quoins, burst pediment above door with coat of arms, dormers, cupola – Book 1

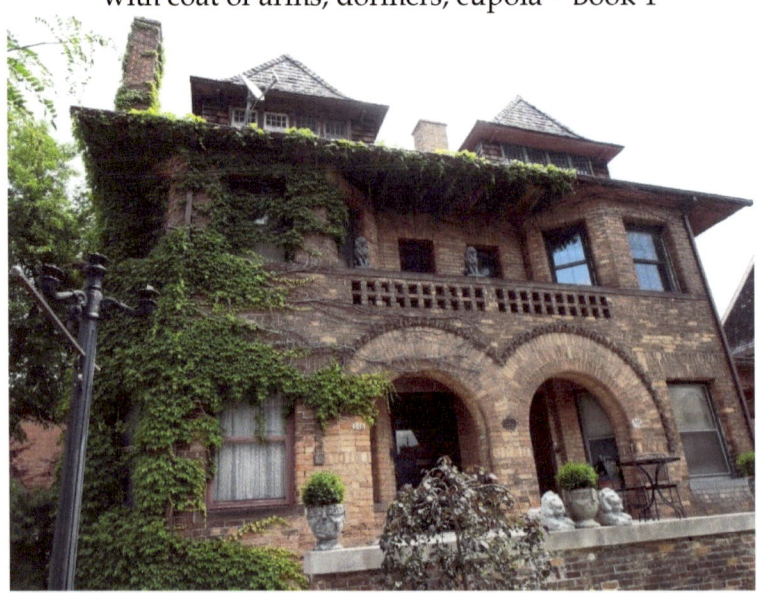

546-548 Devonshire Road built 1890 – Bed & Breakfast - 1889
Romanesque style arched entrances – Book 1

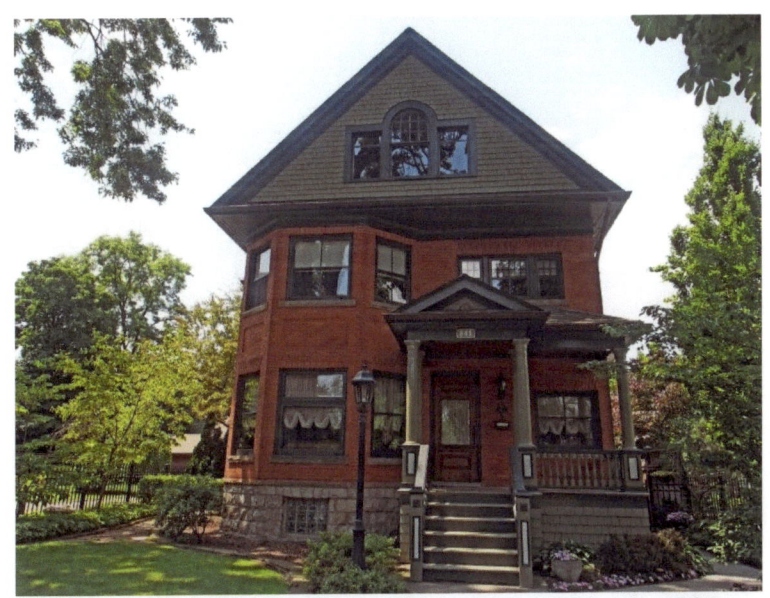

841 Kildare Road – Miers-Fraser House built 1904 – Edwardian, Palladian window, two-storey bay, Ionic columns supporting a pediment – Book 1

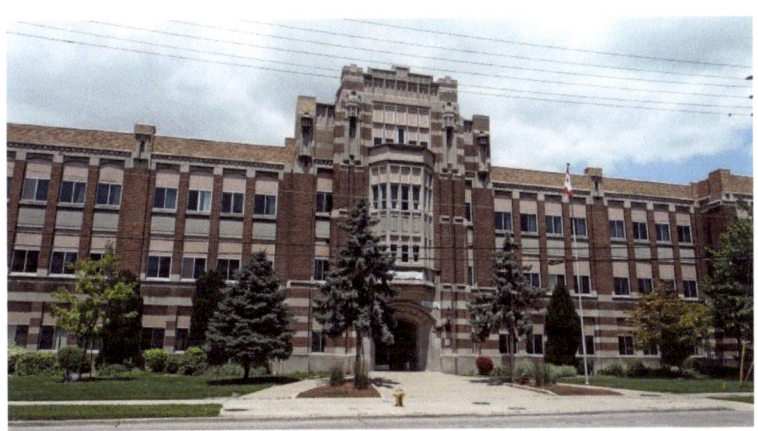

2100 Richmond Street - Walkerville Collegiate – 1922 - Classical Revival style – Book 1

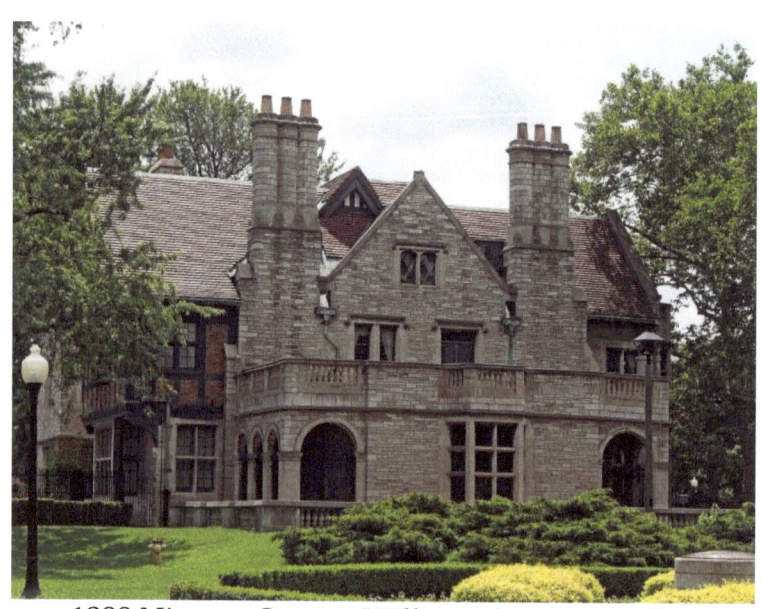

1899 Niagara Street - Willistead Manor – 1906
16th-century Tudor-Jacobean style of an English manor house was commissioned by Edward Chandler Walker, the second son of Hiram Walker. It has 36-rooms but contained only one bedroom. Edward and his wife never had any children, and the coach houses provided ample room for guests. The exterior of gray limestone, quarried in Amherstburg, was hand-cut at the Willistead work site by Scottish stonemasons specifically imported for the project. Tudoresque half-timbering – Book 1

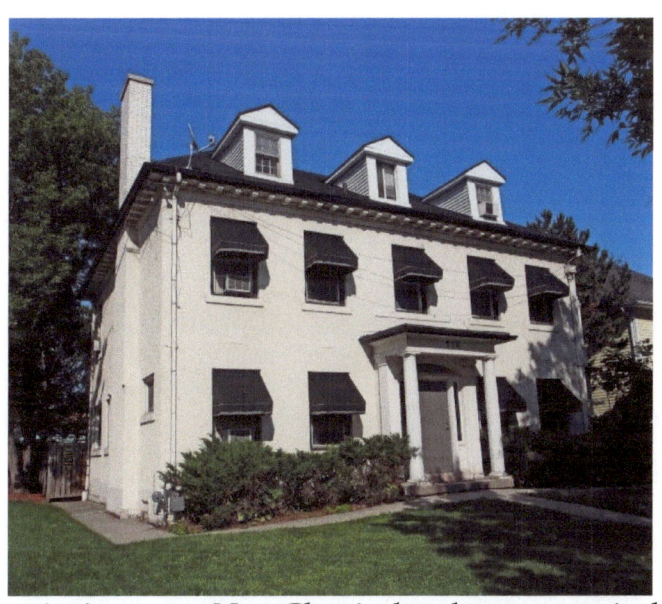

706 Victoria Avenue – Neo-Classical style, symmetrical façade with a prominent columned entry porch sheltering the fanlight and sidelights of the paneled door; dentiled eaves, dormers in attic – Book 2

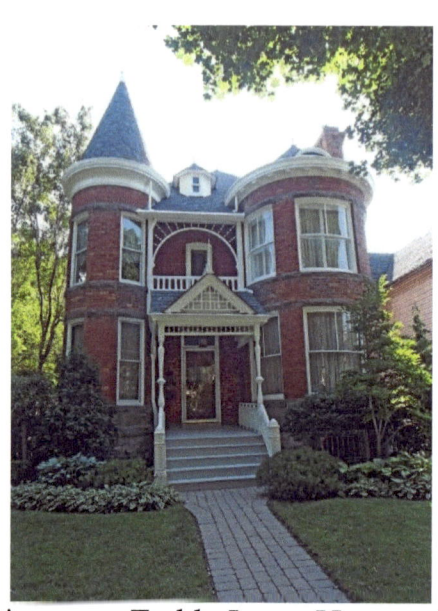

719 Victoria Avenue - Treble-Large House – 1895 - Queen Anne Revival style – Book 2

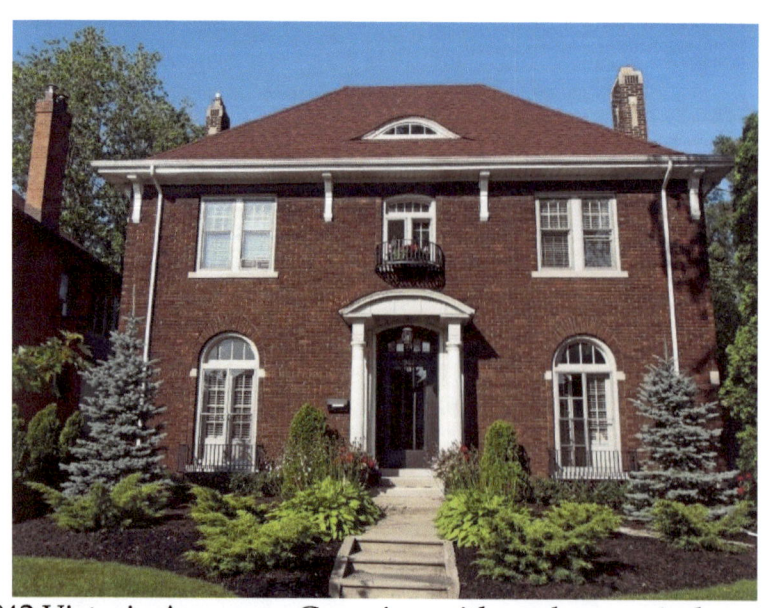

942 Victoria Avenue – Georgian with eyebrow window in roof, pillared entrance with rounded pediment

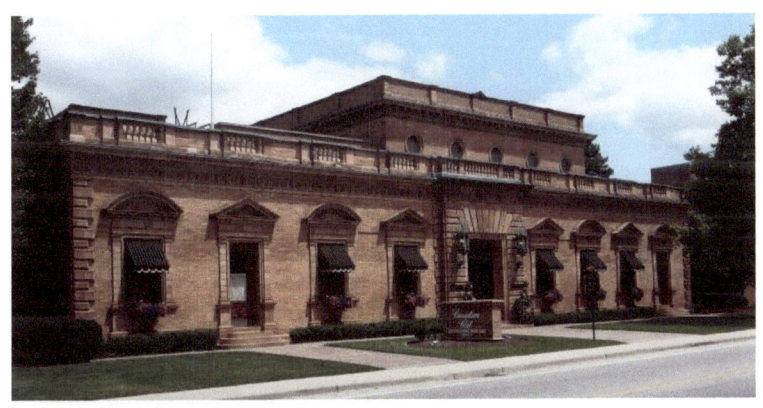

2072 Riverside Drive East – Hiram Walker main office building 1894 – Florentine Renaissance – Book 3

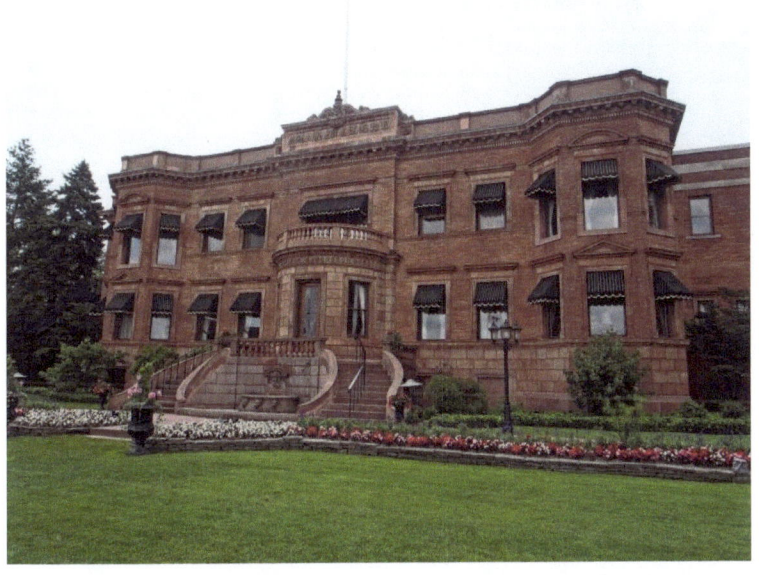

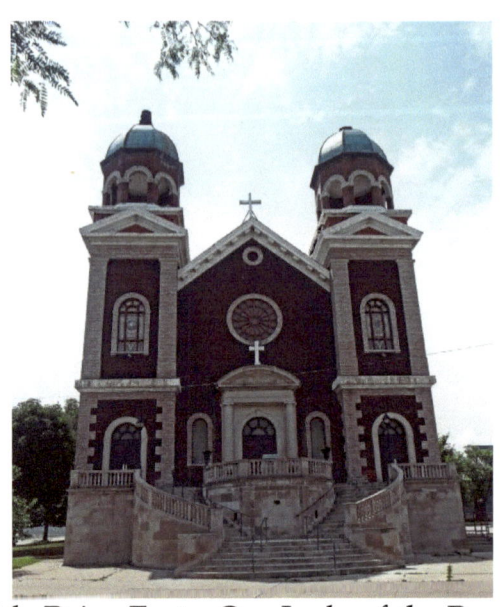

2879 Riverside Drive East – Our Lady of the Rosary Church - built 1907-1913 - Romanesque-style brick and stone building could hold about 1,000 people, features two domed bell towers – Book 3

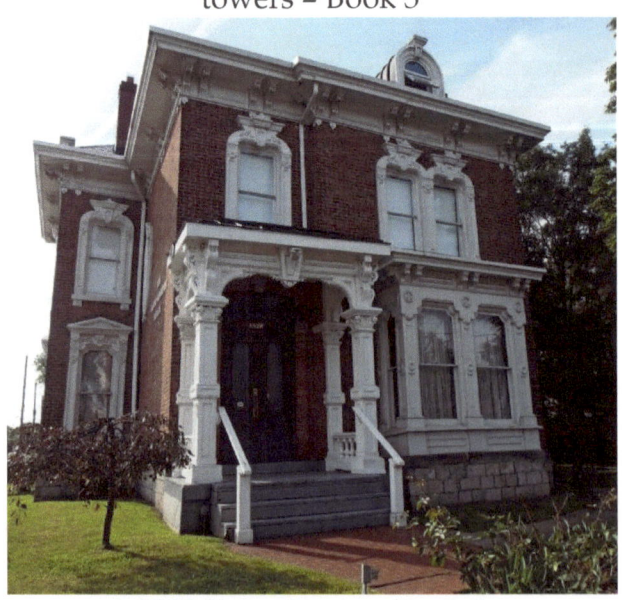

3203 Peter Street – Book 3

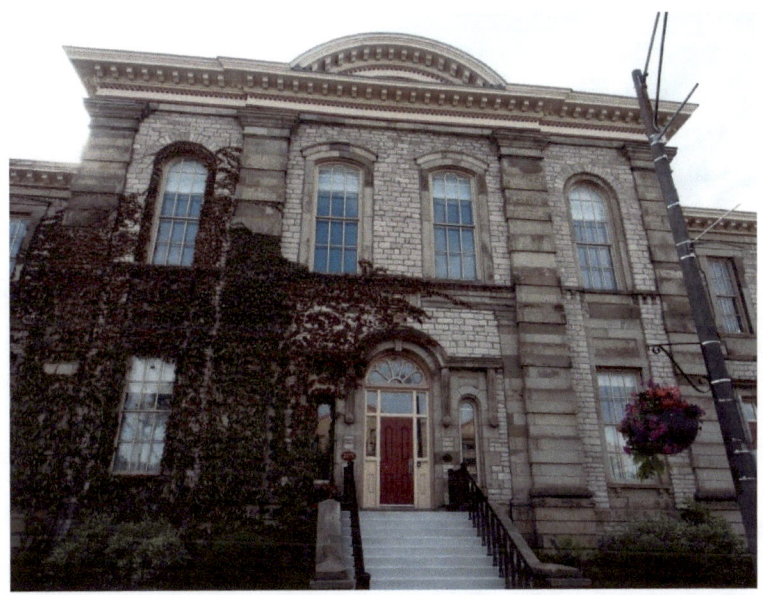

3277 Sandwich Street – Mackenzie Hall – District Court House and Gaol - when–the British withdrew from Detroit in 1796 they transferred the courts of the Western District to Sandwich (Windsor) – this building constructed in 1856 in Renaissance Revival style; a facade broken with pilasters which give strong vertical lines; the main entrance has side lights and a fanlight; it is constructed of Anderdon limestone and Ohio sandstone. The carving above the main doorway represents the seal of the Western District of Upper Canada. – Book 3

Amherstburg, Ontario – My Top 10 Picks

Amherstburg is located near the mouth of the Detroit River in Essex County about twenty-five kilometres south of the United States city of Detroit, Michigan. The British military garrison, Fort Malden, was established here in 1796. The town was developed by Loyalists who were granted land by the Crown in Ontario after the British lost the American Revolutionary War. The Loyalists built many of their houses in the French style of a century before, giving the new town a historic character.

The local public high school in Amherstburg is General Amherst High School and is named after Jeffery Amherst, 1st Baron Amherst of Montreal, who served as an officer in the British Army and as Commander-in-Chief of the Forces. Amherst is best known as the architect of Britain's successful campaign to conquer the territory of New France during the French and Indian War when he led the British attack on Louisbourg on Cape Breton Island in June 1758. Amherst led an army against French troops on Lake Champlain, where he captured Fort Ticonderoga in July 1759, while another army under Sir William Johnson took Niagara also in July 1759, and James Wolfe besieged and eventually captured Quebec with a third army in September 1759.

From July 1760, Amherst led an army down the St. Lawrence River from Fort Oswego, joined with Brigadier Murray from Quebec and Brigadier Haviland from Ill-aux-Noix in a three-way pincer, and captured Montreal, ending French rule in North America on September 8. In recognition of this victory, Amherst was appointed as the first British Governor General in the territories that eventually became Canada.

From his base at New York, Amherst oversaw the dispatch of troops under Monckton and Haviland to take part in British expeditions in the West Indies that led to the British capture of Dominica in 1761 and Martinique and Cuba in 1762.

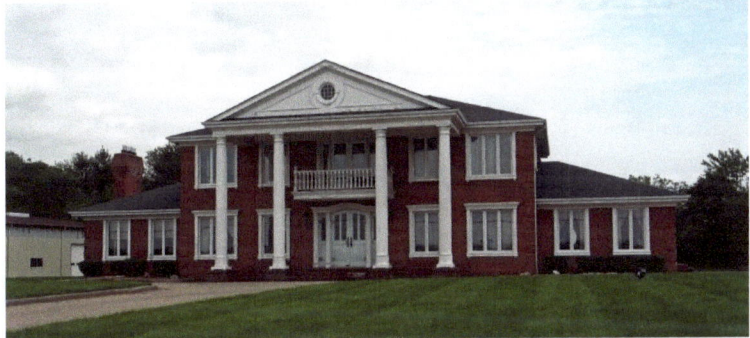

Dalhousie Street – Greek Revival, two-storey Doric pillars, pediment, second floor balcony, side lights – Book 1

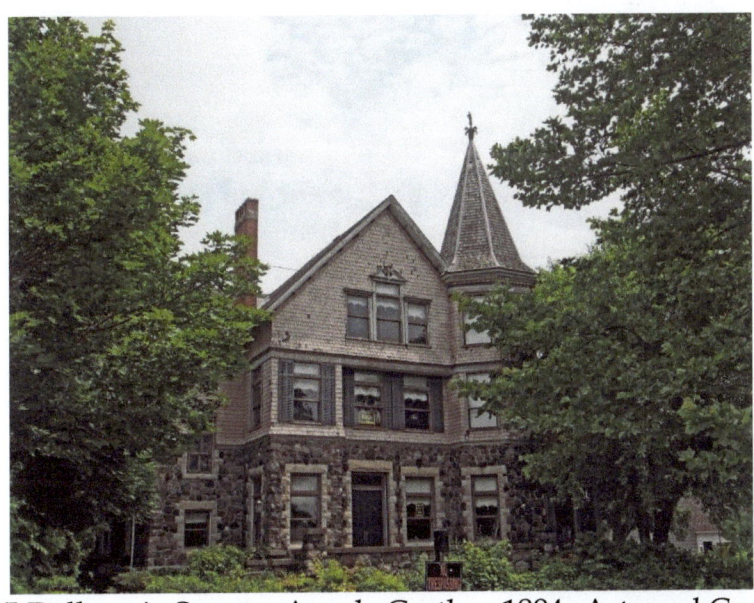

495 Dalhousie Street – Argyle Castle – 1894 -Arts and Crafts style, Palladian style window with window hood, turret – Book 1

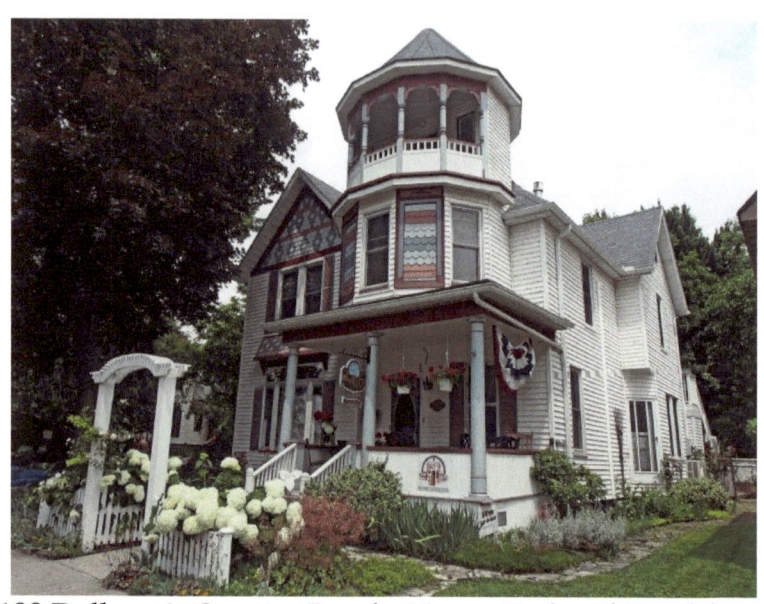

199 Dalhousie Street – Bondy House Bed and Breakfast - Century old Victorian Queen Anne home, turret called "Widow's Walk" for a great view, trichromatic siding – Book 1

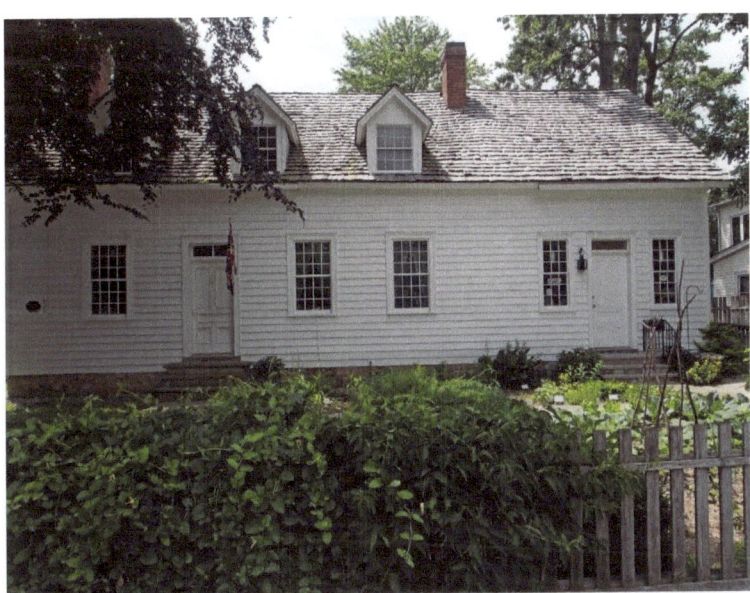

214 Dalhousie Street – Pensioner's cottage - the oldest house in Amherstburg (1796) – moved here from River Rouge, Detroit in 1798 by merchants Leith, Shepherd & Duff; purchased in 1838 by Thomas F. Park and owned by the Park Family (tinsmiths) until 1945 – moved to this site in 1972 and restored by the Rotary Club of Amherstburg as the Park House Museum - very early example of solid log, French frame construction; three dormers, Victorian style – Book 1

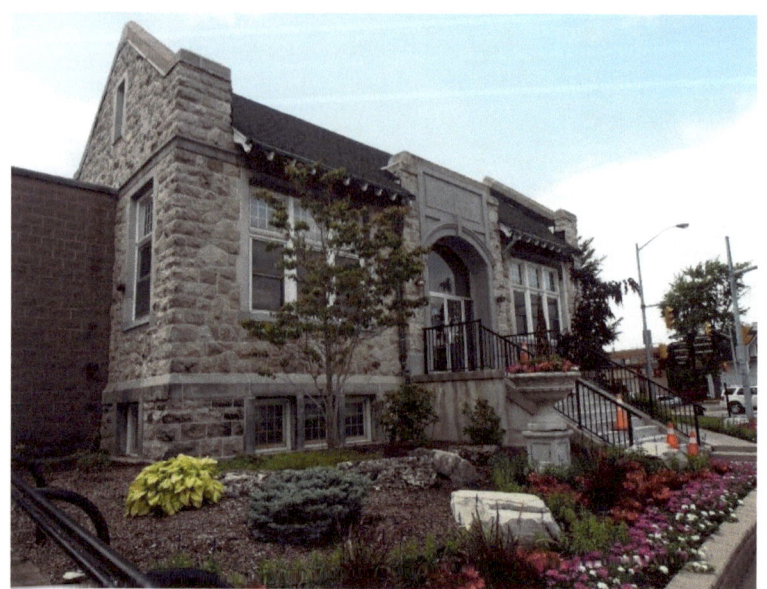

232 Sandwich Street South – Amherstburg Carnegie Public Library – built in 1911 of limestone from the old Huron Indian Quarry in Anderdon Township – Book 1

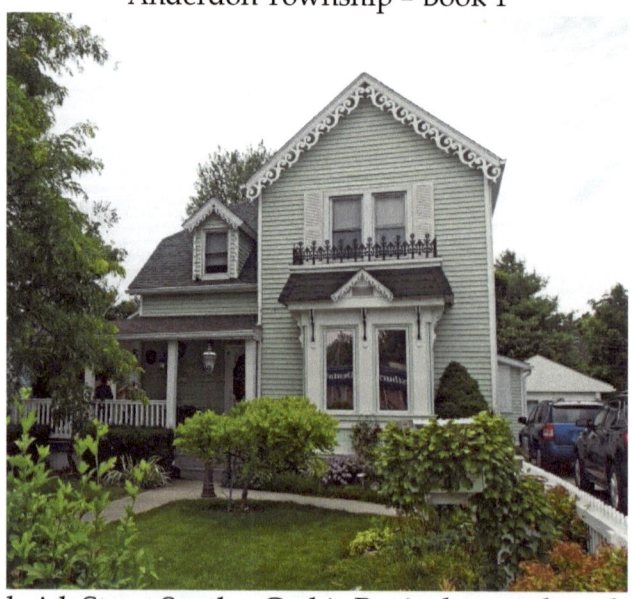

36 Sandwich Street South – Gothic Revival, verge board trim on gable, iron cresting above windows, cornice brackets, dormer above one storey section – Book 2

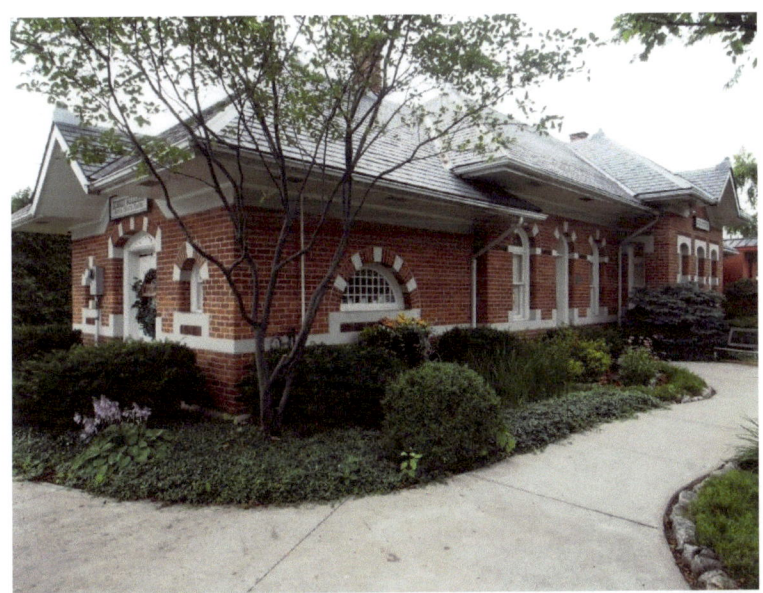

140 Richmond Street – Michigan Central Railway Station – 1892 – dichromatic brickwork – Book 2

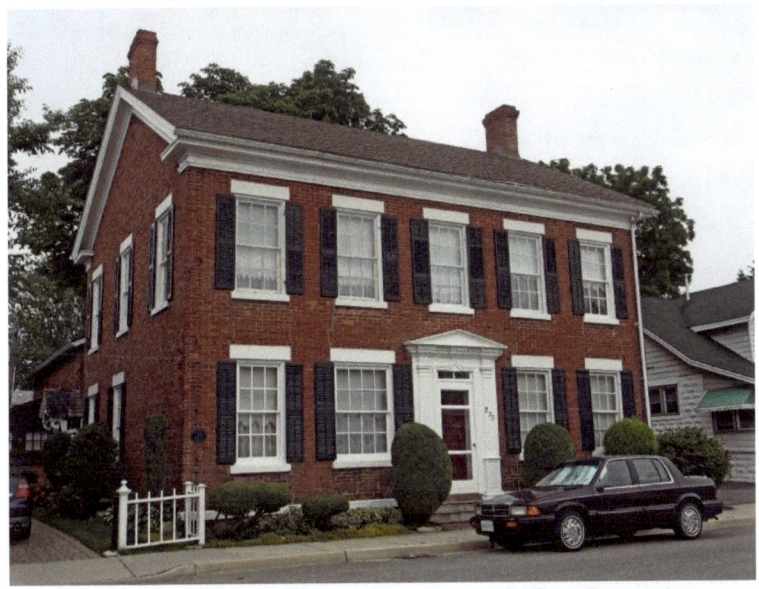

273 Ramsay Street – Dunbar House – 1849 – Georgian – two-storey brick, pediment above doorway with dentil moulding below, transom window – Book 2

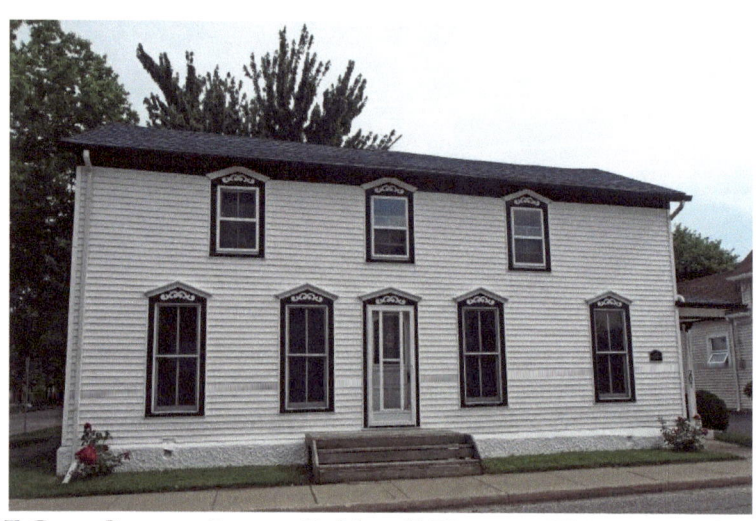

207 Gore Street – James Caldwell House - This original one-storey log house was built between 1835 and 1840 by James Caldwell. Caldwell served with the British Army during the Revolutionary War. At the end of this war, he was given a large tract of land in Amherstburg for his service. Georgian style – Book 2

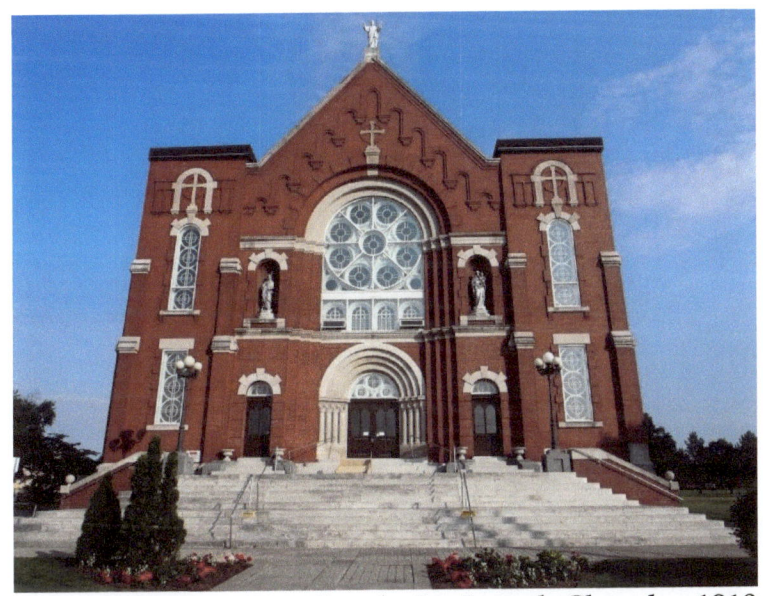

9399 North Town Line Road - St. Joseph Church – 1910 - French-Canadian Church – a landmark at the centre of the former community River Canard - entrance with Corinthian capitals on columns, voussoirs and keystones, decorative brickwork in gable – Book 2

www.ingramcontent.com/pod-product-compliance
Lightning Source LLC
Chambersburg PA
CBHW040225220526
45473CB00001B/129